THE ILLUSTRATED
ENCYCLOPEDIA OF

# VICTORIANA

# THE ILLUSTRATED
# ENCYCLOPEDIA OF
# VICTORIANA

**A COMPREHENSIVE GUIDE TO THE DESIGNS, CUSTOMS, AND INVENTIONS OF THE VICTORIAN ERA**

*Nancy Ruhling & John Crosby Freeman*

## RUNNING PRESS
PHILADELPHIA · LONDON

**A RUNNING PRESS/FRIEDMAN GROUP BOOK**

© 1994 by Michael Friedman Publishing Group, Inc.

9 8 7 6 5 4 3 2 1

Digit on the right indicates the number of this printing.

Library of Congress Cataloging-in-Publication Number 93-87457

ISBN 1-56138-405-4

*THE ILLUSTRATED ENCYCLOPEDIA OF VICTORIANA*
*A Comprehensive Guide to the Designs, Customs, and Inventions of the Victorian Era*
was prepared and produced by
Michael Friedman Publishing Group, Inc.
15 West 26th Street
New York, New York 10010

Editor: Nathaniel Marunas
Art Director: Jeff Batzli
Designer: Tanya Ross-Hughes
Photo Editor: Emilya Naymark

Typeset by Classic Type
Color separation by Ocean Graphic (International) Company Ltd.
Printed and bound in China by Leefung-Asco Printers Ltd.

This book may be ordered from the Publisher.
Please add $2.50 for postage and handling.
*But try your bookstore first.*

Running Press Book Publishers
125 South Twenty-second Street
Philadelphia, Pennsylvania 19103

**DEDICATION**

To Glenn and Jim, who made the Old House home.

——Nancy Ruhling

# Contents

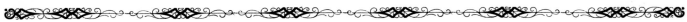

# Introduction

*It is only fitting that the nineteenth century be remembered as the Era of Victoria because at that time the world looked to England for guidance in art, design, and architecture. Although France remained the undisputed leader of* haute couture *and* haute cuisine *during Victoria's reign, it was the English who set all other styles.*

*From the time Victoria was crowned in 1838 until her death in 1901, the Industrial Revolution caused great, lightning-quick changes in the world, particularly in the field of commercial production. Thus, combined with the fact that Victorian society tended to be object-oriented, there were many intriguing items of everyday life, which have since been forgotten. The* Illustrated Encyclopedia of Victoriana *not only defines many of these long-neglected items, but puts them in historical perspective, giving a glimpse —without rose-colored glasses—of what life might have been like when Victoria ruled.*

*To that end, John Crosby Freeman and I have chosen to emphasize the odd and the eclectic flavor of that period of time. During our years at* Victorian Homes *magazine, John and I have fielded hundreds of "what's-it" questions and are now sharing some of the answers*

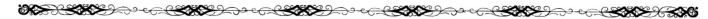

*with you. For this volume, John concentrated on the exterior decoration of house and garden, and I focused on interior and personal decoration. The Illustrated Encyclopedia of Victoriana is comprehensive, but by no means complete. Entire volumes can and have been written on each of the entries chosen. Instead, this book can be read cover to cover or be used as a reference work to look up various items as the need arises.*

*I believe that Victoria would be amused and even amazed by* The Illustrated Encyclopedia of Victoriana—*I hope you will be too.*

*—Nancy A. Ruhling*
*Huntington, New York*
*Feb. 13, 1993*

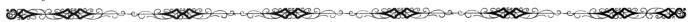

## ABBOTSFORD

Sir Walter Scott translated his poetic penchant for Gothic romances and his love of antiquities into real life by building Abbotsford, a great baronial residence set upon an English moor. A decade in the making, Abbotsford was completed in 1824. Articles about it increased interest in the Gothic Revival style and set design precedents that lasted for decades. Where possible, Scott used fragments of medieval antiquities in its construction, and when he couldn't find originals, he had them antiqued. It is to Scott, the author of the verses in *Ivanhoe* and the "Lay of the Last Minstrel," that the Victorians owed not only their interest in the Gothic style, but also the decorating schemes for their libraries and their insistence upon crimson wallpaper in dining rooms.

## ACANTHUS LEAVES

Perhaps no other decorative symbol is so associated with the arts of the Victorian period as the acanthus leaf. It is possible to find the carved leaves of this prickly Mediterranean herb scrolling themselves around the curves of nearly every style of nineteenth-century furniture, except some of the later ones.

## AESTHETIC MOVEMENT

An essentially British attitude toward the decorative arts, the Aesthetic Movement was a Victorian attempt to employ a self-consciously "artistic" approach to the design of everyday items, primarily in order to take market share away from French manufacturers who at that time dominated important industries, including ceramics, textiles, furniture, and wallpaper—in short, the fashion industry itself. The opening of Japan to world trade in the 1850s was the spark that ignited the Aesthetic Movement. Here was a civilization that had successfully elevated the making of domestic artifacts to the level of exercises in pure design. During the 1870s and 1880s "Art" was added as a fashionable (if pretentious) prefix to the names of all kinds of decorative art, especially those with a Japonesque flavor. By the 1870s the Aesthetic Movement involved the synthesis of day-to-day practicality and fanciful adornment; the result was the application of elaborate surface decoration to household items such as butter churns, flatirons, rolling pins, and workbenches. In addition, many of these newly decorated items were introduced into more elegant settings, including parlors, dining rooms, and hallways. It is interesting to note that the same thing happened a century later in the 1970s when the American Country movement saw a similar conversion and redistribution of barnyard antiques such as egg crates and milk cans.

**LEFT:** *Acanthus leaves ornament this bracketed shelf.* **OPPOSITE PAGE:** *Abbotsford, Sir Walter Scott's impressive residence, was a tribute to the Gothic idiom. This room, which is decorated with trophies of the hunt, of suits armor, and plenty of elaborate woodwork (note the detail in the Gothic Revival alcoves that house the armor), is typical of the ostentatious baronial manor.*

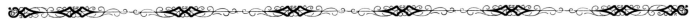

# AESTHETIC MOVEMENT COSTUME

When speaking of clothing that was advocated by followers of the Aesthetic Movement, "costume" is the most appropriate word to use. The pre-Raphaelite painters changed the face of beauty by painting women, like the stunning Jane Morris, in long, flowing robes. These high-waisted gowns, which had sleeves that puffed out at the shoulders, harked back to the fourteenth century. Although there is much evidence that few people followed the style, women of artistic bent were advised to wear such gowns in colors of dull or sage greens, peacock blues and dull rich reds, or mellow amber yellows, perhaps decorated with an embroidered peacock feather, calla lily, or sunflower. The style rules for personal and interior decoration were the same among the Aesthetics, and upholstery fabrics were even recommended for these costumes.

Oscar Wilde was the model for men's fashion of the Aesthetic Movement, lounging languidly in his velvet knickerbocker suit, a lily in its buttonhole. His visit to the United States inspired the story "Little Lord Fauntleroy" and the little-boy sissy suit of the same name.

# ALBERT, THE PRINCE CONSORT

To those who weren't on familiar terms with him, he was known as Augustus Albert Emmanuel; to Queen Victoria, his wife, he was known as "my angel." And if he was not exactly the power behind the throne, he was at least a powerful influence upon it. Victoria, who didn't really like the job of ruling, depended upon him as her most trusted adviser and private secretary. Albert really had a tough time of it all, because not only did he, by law, have to play second fiddle to his wife, he was literally on foreign soil. Born on August 26, 1819, near Coburg, Germany, he was never really accepted by the English public, even though Victoria was his first cousin. From the time he married

Victoria in 1840 until he died prematurely and quite suddenly in 1861, the queen depended upon him when it came to matters of taste. He set out to educate her—and England—about art and music, and took over the tasks of renovating and decorating their palaces.

The Crystal Palace Exhibition of 1851, a tribute to the world's and England's achievements in every field, was Albert's idea. Throughout his life, he continued to promote advances in art, architecture, industry, and science.

# ALBUM QUILTS

The finest examples of Victorian quilting in America, many of which are now enthroned in art museums, were the early Victorian appliqué "album" or "friendship" quilts, so named because they constituted albums of unique squares each made, and often signed, by a different woman. These extraordinary quilts were given not only in friendship, but often as a wedding gift. Early Victorian sewing circles also made them to raise money for their churches or for other worthy causes.

## ANAGLYPTA

A heavily embossed paper-pulp product, anaglypta was the most popular of the scores of Lincrusta imitations that flooded the market when that wallcovering became successful. Patented in 1887, anaglypta was not as durable as Lincrusta, but was cheaper and easier to install. It is still being made.

Anaglypta ® Crown Berger Ltd.

## ANIMAL LEGS AND PAWS

Victorian furniture, if studied carefully, often has a humorous aspect. The furniture legs just had to be decorative, and when cabinetmakers got bored with those French-looking cabriole legs, they turned to paws of all sorts. George Hunzinger, for instance, made some parlor suites in the 1860s and 1870s with hooved feet that made the pieces look like they were about to gallop off at any moment. Furniture with ball-and-claw feet didn't appear until about the 1890s, after the Colonial Revival style made its patriotic appearance.

🟦 **OPPOSITE PAGE:** *Quilting bees allowed women not only to show off their sewing skills but to socialize with friends.* **ABOVE:** *Anaglypta had a textured look that made walls look like they were covered in expensive hand-tooled leather and was so easy to keep clean that it was placed in many high-traffic areas, such as entrance halls and dining rooms.* **ABOVE, RIGHT:** *Victorian cabinetmakers often used animal motifs, including paws, as decorative elements. Symbols of the hunt were common in the dining room.*

## ANNUALS

"To the annuals, we are indebted mainly for our brightest and best flowers in the late summer and autumn months. Without the Phlox, and Petunia, and Portulaca, and Aster, and Stock, our autumn gardens would be poor indeed, and how we would miss the sweet fragrance of the Alyssum, Mignonette, and Sweet Pea, if any ill-luck should deprive us of these old favorites," stated *Vick's Flower and Vegetable Garden* (1878). Other varieties listed by Vick's were ageratum, amaranthus (love-lies-bleeding), antirrhinum (snapdragon), balsam, calendula (marigold), calliopsis (beautiful eye), canna, candytuft, catchfly, celosia (cockscomb), centaurea, cleome (Rocky Mountain bee plant), clarkia, delphinium, California poppy, helianthus (sunflower), lupin, pansy, poppy, rincinus (castor oil bean), salvia, verbena, vinca, and zinnia.

**ABOVE:** *During the last century, arches or series of arches called arcades were often used on public buildings to create open spaces.*
**OPPOSITE PAGE:** *The application of a stylized portrait to the back of a chair gives the piece a decorative focal point.*

## ANTIMACASSAR

"So's your antimacassar" was a phrase that was always good for a laugh during the Jazz Age of the 1920s because it symbolized to Flaming Youth the absurdity of genteel Victorian customs; besides, the word sounded funny. Antimacassars were decorative, anti-soil textiles that were attached to the arms, backs, and headrests of expensively upholstered furniture. Headrests were most vulnerable to the Macassar oil from Celebes Island (in the Malay archipelago) that Victorian gentlemen used as hair oil. The necessity for an antimacassar reveals the double standard of Victorian behavior, for gentlemen were permitted to lounge their (oil-slicked) heads against the headrests of chairs and women were not. A term more generally in use during the Victorian age was "chair tidy," which was usually a form of "home art" needlework.

## APPLIED ORNAMENT

On Victorian furniture, "applied ornament" refers to a small hand- or machine-carved decorative piece that is applied to the body of the finished piece. Many Renaissance Revival pieces, for example, have round or oval applied ornaments in the form of female faces.

## APPLIQUÉ QUILTS

The aristocracy of Victorian quilted bedspreads was the appliquéd or patched quilt. The appliqué process, in which irregularly shaped pieces of cloth are sewn on a background textile, permits more curvilinear and pictorial designs than the pieced quilt. Victorian appliqué quilts tend to be the best preserved, are made of the finest textiles, and display the highest level of craftsmanship.

## AQUARIA

One of the most impressive "rustic adornments for homes of taste" was the aquarium—a glass-enclosed, underwater garden with fish, sometimes supported by an elaborate metal frame and situated on a magnificent stand.

## ARCHES/ARCADES

"An arcade, or series of arches, is perhaps one of the most beautiful objects attached to the buildings of a city which architecture affords," according to Joseph Gwilt in his *Encyclopedia of Architecture* (1842–1867). Designers of Victorian commercial buildings and their clients heartily agreed with this statement. The Victorian technologies of cast-iron and cast-concrete were used to construct and attach stacks of arcades to factories, warehouses, stores, and office buildings, usually setting them within colonnades of the same material to balance the vertical and horizontal forces of the facade. In the 1870s a manufacturer named Ransome was selling "artificial stone" concrete arches in Chicago. The first office building constructed after the Chicago Fire was the Delaware Building (1871). This recently restored building has the first cast-concrete skin in the United States and features arcades within colonnades, including typical late Victorian Italianate "basket-handle" arches in the fourth and seventh floors. Cast-iron arcades within colonnades are also featured in Daniel Badger's *Illustrations of Iron Architecture* (1865).

# ARCHITECTURAL ILLUSTRATIONS

During the nineteenth century, successful architectural firms employed artist-architects and architectural draughtsmen to create beautifully drawn and splendidly watercolored elevations and perspectives. Many were anonymous itinerants, following the ebb and flow of building booms. The architectural sketchbook and view-book, another class of architectural illustration, were collections of lithographs of the buildings of distant places and times that were made available to architects unable to inspect the originals. Archives of architectural drawings and libraries of architectural books are safely protected, but the recent enthusiasm for these illustrations as works of art jeopardizes the survival of what remains in private hands. Plans, working drawings, specifications, contracts, correspondence, and book texts are among the important records so endangered.

# ARCHITECTURAL ORDERS

Illustrations and descriptions of the Five Architectural Orders (Doric, Ionic, Corinthian, Composite, Tuscan) had been published at the beginning of neoclassical architectural books since the Renaissance, but they disappeared from American builder's guides and architectural pattern-books in the 1850s. Superficially, this indicated that the Victorian battle of styles between Greek and Gothic or classical and romantic had resulted in the victory of romanticism over neoclassicism. In actuality, romanticism had energized American neoclassicism since 1780, when Thomas Jefferson emulated an ancient Roman temple from the period of the Republic for the new Virginia State Capitol at Richmond. Furthermore, neoclassicism survived as a viable architectural language throughout the nineteenth century, especially in the cornice-frieze-architrave relationships of neoclassical entablature.

# ARCHITECTURAL PATTERNBOOKS/ MAIL-ORDER ARCHITECTURE

Architectural illustrations and books published since the beginning of the Renaissance functioned to some extent as advertisements for their designers and authors, but it was Victorian entrepreneurs in the United States who converted the genteel tradition of neoclassical architectural publishing into the bourgeois marketplace for mail-order building designs. Greek Revival builder's guides published in the 1820s and 1830s, especially those by Asher Benjamin, implied a willingness to supply drawings for elevations, plans, and details of buildings for sites unseen. The same was true of the romantic stylebooks of A. J. Downing and the patternbooks of William Ranlett in the 1840s. Finally, in 1856, New York architects Cleaveland and Backus announced in the romantic stylebook *Village and Farm Cottages* that "For the convenience of such as may wish to build after any of the design in this work, the Authors have prepared careful, lithographed working drawings and printed specifications for each. These comprise every thing necessary to enable any competent workman fully to understand the plans. They will be forwarded, together with blank forms of contract by mail, on receipt of a special application, and remittance." Thus began the U.S. industry of mail-order house design, which continues to flourish in the late twentieth century. The most successful Victorian mail-order architectural firm was New York's Palliser & Palliser, which supplied a complete range of domestic, commercial, and civic buildings for the United States, Canada, and South America in the 1880s.

## ARCHITECTURAL PROFESSIONALISM

Nowhere was the establishment of architecture as a profession more of a struggle than in Victorian America. The difficult process began with the British émigré architect Benjamin Henry Latrobe in 1800 and continued throughout the nineteenth century. In the beginning, the issue centered around whether the master builders or the architects controlled the building contracts and building trades. Although several excellent architects rose out of the building trades, qualified architects were frequently confounded with builders, many of whom added an honorific "Architect" to their names. After the Civil War, several professional organizations and professional magazines were established, mostly in the 1870s. The earliest professional courses in architecture were offered at the Massachusetts Institute of Technology (1865), the University of Illinois (1868), Cornell University (1871), Syracuse University (1873), and Columbia University (1881). During the 1890s, eight more institutions founded schools of architecture.

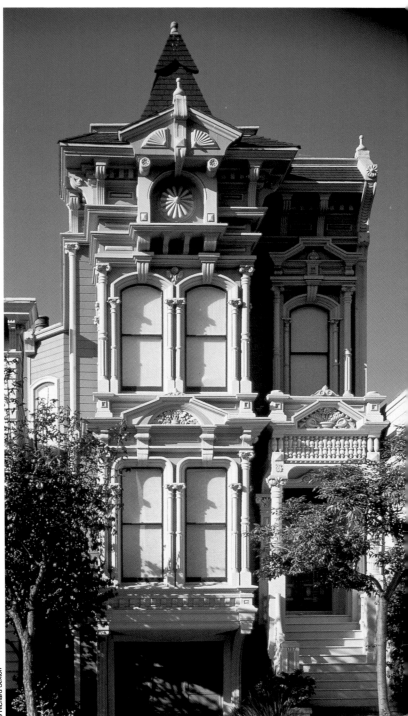

**OPPOSITE PAGE:** *The ubiquitous acanthus leaf decorates the capital, architrave, and frieze of this neoclassical column.* **BELOW:** *As this house in California shows, the Victorians took an exuberant interest in architecture that affected the designs of private dwellings and municipal buildings alike. Architectural details distinguish the exterior of the Victorian house.*

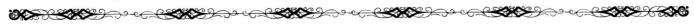

# ARCHITECTURAL SCULPTURE

Despite their intellectual enthusiasm for the glorious architectural sculpture of antiquity and the Renaissance, Victorian Americans rarely converted it into a tangible form capable of providing employment for a large number of sculptors. Much of the demand for architectural sculpture was satisfied by manufactured low-relief sculpture in cast-iron, pressed metal, cast-concrete, terra-cotta, and plaster. Major civil buildings, such as city halls, courthouses, and capitols, often displayed considerable amounts of architectural sculpture, but the main sculptural feature of such buildings usually was a freestanding, colossal figure cast in bronze placed on top of a tower or dome (instead of many large areas of low-relief sculpture).

# ARCHITECTURAL TECHNOLOGY

Since 1941, when Sigfried Giedion published his *Space, Time and Architecture*, those aspects of Victorian technology that could be linked to the development of a modern American architecture—especially the skyscraper—have been extravagantly studied and discussed. These aspects include cast-iron, steel-frame, float glass, portland cement, ferro-concrete, prefabrication, and the elevator. One modern viewpoint romanticizes handcraftsmanship and despises anything done during the Victorian period that rendered it obsolete. Victorian reactions to the development of Victorian architectural technology are rarely sought, but it would be safe to guess that they would not differ much from the concerns of people today: Will it put me out of a job? Will it make my work or life easier? Will it save me money? From this perspective, the greatest developments in Victorian architectural technology were central heating, artificial lighting, indoor plumbing, refrigeration, and flyscreens. An interesting case is offered by the invention in 1832 of balloon framing by one George

Snow in Chicago. During the Victorian period, it helped "win the West" by providing a technology for the economical use of machined lumber in reasonably priced, easily built, and sturdy homes.

# ARGAND BURNER

The Frenchman Aimé Argand (1775–1803) invented this lighting device in the 1780s, but it was Benjamin Franklin and Thomas Jefferson who actually carried examples of this new product across the Atlantic, when they returned from a trip to Paris. The Argand burner, which burned whale or colza oil, allowed air to circulate to the inner and the outer surface of a tubular wick. With the addition of a glass shade, both combustion and the quality of light improved dramatically. Moreover, Argand burners weren't smoky like other lamps of the period.

# ARMCHAIRS

Victorian society perpetuated the ancient association of armchairs with thrones, and therefore reserved the use of the former for men. In fact, during the crinoline era, which coincided more or less with the reign of Napoleon III (1852–1870), women were unable to sit in armchairs because of the voluminous skirts they wore. Victorian systems of shorthand and the invention of the typewriter provided employment for increasing numbers of women during the late nineteenth century, but those secretaries had to sit in armless chairs while male office-workers sat in "office" chairs—chairs with arms.

◆ **ABOVE:** *Purity may have been considered a virtue in women during the last century, but it certainly wasn't practiced in interior or exterior decoration. The Victorians were known for combining design elements from many periods, thus the classical statue, urns, and moldings combined with "modern" details on this house in San Francisco, California.* **OPPOSITE PAGE:** *The armchair was the home furnishing that most clearly pointed out the separation of men and women in the Victorian era.*

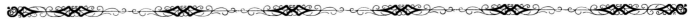

**ABOVE:** *The "balloon-back" chair, which did not have arms, was a standard feature in the Victorian parlor and often in the bedroom. Armless chairs were made specifically for women to accommodate their voluminous gowns and to show that they played second fiddle to men, who sat in commanding armchairs.*
**OPPOSITE PAGE:** *Victorian architecture frequently revived and synthesized earlier styles, a trend that continued well into the twentieth century. This is evident in many of the public institutions built during and after the Victorian era, including the Philadelphia Museum of Art, a Greco-Roman construction built in 1919 and opened to the public in 1928.*

Subsequently, slimmer skirts made it possible for women to fit into late Victorian armchairs. This was acceptable only in places where the patriarchy was not threatened—on the veranda (in rocking chairs with wide seats) and in the library (in chairs with shortened arms).

## ARMLESS CHAIRS

A short vocabulary of terms for armless early Victorian chairs has been developed during the twentieth century by auctioneers, antique dealers, and decorators: "balloon-back," "camel-back," "cameo-back," and "corset-back." The legions of more common Victorian armless chairs have not yet acquired the rarity and value necessary to inspire a specialized vocabulary, but they are important social indicators and should be cataloged as such. Published catalogs of late Victorian chair manufacturers like the Brooklyn Chair Company are sparsely worded, but one catalog from 1887 reveals that the difference between a cottage chair and a dining chair was the addition to the latter of vestigial arms in the upper corners between the seat and chair back to strengthen its weakest point, which was most likely to be broken by boorish "tilting back." Today's owners of Victorian homes too often make the mistake of furnishing them with rare, high-style, and expensive chairs, ignoring the much cheaper common chairs, which are also easier to restore.

## ART FURNITURE

Charles Locke Eastlake (1836–1906) did not invent the concept of late Victorian Art Furniture, for the first Art Furniture company and the first masterpiece of Art Furniture—E. W. Godwin's Japonesque ebonized-wood sideboard now in London's Victoria and Albert Museum—appeared in 1867, the same year Eastlake's *Hints on House-*

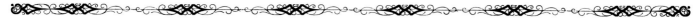

hold *Taste in Furniture, Upholstery and Other Details* was published. Nonetheless, *Household Taste* became one of the most influential books of the Aesthetic Movement, appearing in four London editions from 1867 to 1878 and six Boston editions from 1872 to 1879. It was echoed in Clarence Cook's *The House Beautiful* (1877) and Harriet Prescott Spofford's *Art Decoration Applied to Furniture* (1878). Eastlake condemned the fashionable furniture, calling his time "the age of upholstery," criticizing its "extravagance of *contour*," false use of veneer, dependence on glue, and obliteration of structure by carved ornament. The merry band of "art improvers" were nothing if not patriots, however, for what Eastlake really disliked was French furniture. He preferred furniture in the English tradition, which for him meant furniture of the Gothic Revival. Bruce J. Talbert (1838–1881) made Eastlake's ideas more coherent in *Gothic Forms Applied to Furniture* (1867) and *Examples of Ancient & Modern Furniture* (1876), which were reprinted in Boston in 1873 and 1877, respectively. Art Furniture also encompassed Anglo-Japanese, Queen Anne, Tudor, and Jacobean. United in their dislike of mahogany, veneer, glue, and curves, late Victorian designers of Art Furniture were the precursors of such early twentieth-century furniture designers as Frank Lloyd Wright and Gustav Stickley.

# ART GALLERIES/SCHOOLS/ MUSEUMS

Many of the best places to find examples of the fine arts of painting and sculpture created during the Victorian period are in Philadelphia—especially The Pennsylvania Academy of Fine Arts, designed by Frank Furness, which was completed in time for the 1876 Centennial. The creative use of building materials, surface textures, colors, sculptures, ornamentation, and masculine massing renders the building more than a place for the display and teaching of

fine arts; the structure is itself a dissertation on the fine art of architecture. One of the treasures of American painting located inside is the self-portrait of Charles Willson Peale, *The Artist in His Museum* (1823), on the second floor of Independence Hall. In the painting, Peale lifts a curtain in the baroque manner to reveal his portraits of famous Americans lined up above cases of stuffed American birds and animals in a room dominated by a mastodon skeleton he excavated. The portrait is a concise visual summation of the roles of exhibition space, wherein art, science, history, and curiosities are presented with simple showmanship. An influential alternative architecture for an art gallery was the Art Gallery of the Centennial Exhibition in Fairmount Park, now called Memorial Hall. It was the prototype for the Art Institute of Chicago (1892), the Milwaukee Public Museum (1893), the Brooklyn Museum (1893), and the main facade of the Metropolitan Museum of Art (1895).

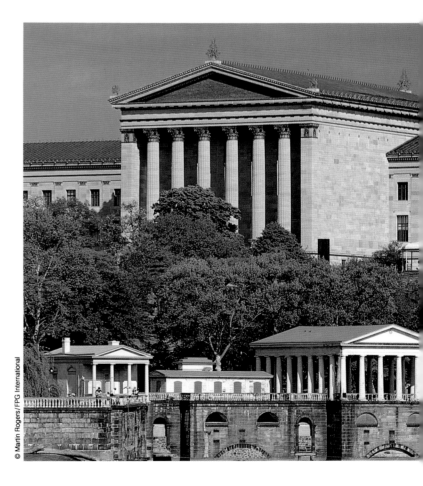
© Martin Rogers/FPG International

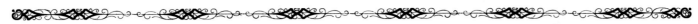

© Richard Sexton

abstract the best qualities of all historic glassmaking as the basis for a unique style that would endure for centuries. At the end of the nineteenth century, it was co-opted by Art Nouveau and disappeared in the vulgarizations of that style in the 1920s. Christopher Dresser's Clutha glass, like other kinds of art glassware made during the 1880s and 1890s, had a surface quality best described as antiquity recently unearthed. This is why iridescent effects were much admired, as in Louis Comfort Tiffany's Favrile glass. Art glass had more impact on late Victorian interior decoration in the form of leaded-glass windows where the rich lights of their transmitted colors dazzled all who beheld them. Tiffany's windows are the most famous, but John La Farge (1835–1910) was the greatest American artist of the period to work in the medium. His first great commission was in 1878 for the windows of H.H. Richardson's Holy Trinity Episcopal Church in Boston. In 1879 LaFarge also held a patent on making opalescent glass.

## ARTISTS' STUDIOS

During the last quarter of the nineteenth century, the public became quite interested not only in art but in artists' houses. Many successful artists were considered celebrities and had incomes to match. Their houses, which, of course, always contained studios, were not merely places to work and entertain VIPs and royalty. The studio was part salesroom and part picture gallery. Once a year, in England at least, these studios were opened to the public. Many artists began using their studios as the subject for paintings, which intrigued the public to such an extent that even those who couldn't paint started imitating the decoration, which tended to be rather bohemian and Japonesque.

## ART GLASS

By the 1870s, all components of interior decoration were available in "art" varieties based on one of the design vocabularies favored by the Aesthetic Movement: Gothic Revival, Japonesque, antiquity, and folk medieval. As with other "art manufacturers," late Victorian manufacturers of art glass strove for simplicity, honest expression of materials, obvious construction, excellent craftsmanship, and superior knowledge of design. They neither copied historic glass nor pandered to vulgar taste, but attempted to

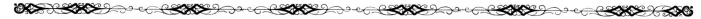

## ART NEEDLEWORK

Like other forms of late Victorian "art manufacture," art needlework distinguished itself from "fancy work" by a high-minded approach to design. The most influential organization in Britain was the New Kensington School of Art in London, assisted by Burne-Jones, Walter Crane, and William Morris. Kensington embroidery from the Royal School of Art Needlework was exhibited at the 1876 Philadelphia Centennial, where it inspired Candace Wheeler

**OPPOSITE PAGE:** *Art-glass windows not only introduced rainbows of color into rooms, but were often employed to block unsightly views. Louis Comfort Tiffany and John La Farge elevated art-glass works into fine art.* **ABOVE:** *While lower-class women spent their time mending clothes, women of the more monied classes, who had leisure time on their hands, created all kinds of art needlework to decorate every room of the house.*

(1827–1923) to form in 1877 The Society of Decorative Art in New York, with the assistance of Samuel Coleman and Louis Comfort Tiffany. In addition to the Kensington revival of ancient English embroidery, the Society of Decorative Art revived the American tradition of eighteenth- and early nineteenth-century Bethlehem embroidery, flower embroidery made and taught by Moravians at Bethlehem, Pennsylvania, and elsewhere. "The result was an immediate resort to stains and silks and flosses, wherewith larger and more important things than tidies were created—lambrequins, hangings, bedspreads, screens, and many other furnishings, all wrought in exquisite flosses, and more or less beautiful in color." The impact of art needlework was far greater in the United States (where it was enthusiastically promoted by makers of embroidery threads as a way to achieve artistic self-fulfillment) than in Britain (where it was justified as useful employment for "unfortunate sisters, who were rather malodorously called decayed gentlewomen").

## ART NOUVEAU

Although the origins of Art Nouveau can be traced to the ideas and works of England's William Morris and his followers, it was Samuel Bing's Salon de l'Art Nouveau in Paris that not only gave the name to this so-called modern style in 1895, but provided it with its first real forum. Bing's salon was devoted to exhibiting works of contemporary designers, painters, and sculptors—anything that was, in essence, modern. Art Nouveau didn't last much beyond 1905 and never achieved a wide popularity. A reaction against the angularity of mass production, Art Nouveau emphasized the sinuous line—the organic form of flowers like the lily, the iris, and the orchid, for instance. More than a style, Art Nouveau embodied the idea that art could express something new and modern to salute the new, modern century.

Indeed, although Art Nouveau sprang up in several countries, almost the only element these outcroppings had in common was the name—and even that varied. It was called Art Nouveau and Modern Style in France; Modernism in Spain; *Moderne Stile* in Italy; and *Jugendstil* in Germany. And although its sinuous lines rarely showed up in architecture or furniture, they did predominate in the decorative arts.

## ARTS & CRAFTS MOVEMENT

Named for the Arts & Crafts Exhibition Society of 1888, the Arts & Crafts Movement was founded by John Ruskin and William Morris, who preached that craft was art, as exemplified by works of the Middle Ages. A reaction against the shoddy machine-made objects that were being churned out during the Industrial Revolution, this movement, which was distinctly American, changed the way the decorative arts were perceived. Furniture and decorative accessories were to be handcrafted and of simple, nature-inspired design, sturdy construction, and excellent quality. Although everything was supposed to be handmade, this wasn't always the case. Machines had their uses, the movement found; some objects were even made to look as though they had been handcrafted.

The movement was about more than decoration; it was also a philosophy of domestic life that attempted to elevate the role of the worker, bring him beauty and personal satisfaction, and improve not only working conditions but his lot in general. Several communities were established in country settings to carry out this ideal. Gustav Stickley, who coined the term "craftsman," which soon became a synonym for a designer of the Arts & Crafts Movement, set up his company, United Crafts (later called Craftsman Workshops), near Syracuse, New York. And Elbert Hubbard settled his guildlike Roycroft Shops in East Aurora, New York.

Other key players in the Arts & Crafts Movement, which lasted until about 1920, included Dirk Van Erp, Charles Sumner Greene, who formed a company with his brother, Henry Mather Greene, and Prairie School architects Louis Sullivan and Frank Lloyd Wright.

## ASTRAL LAMP

The astral lamp, patented in France in 1809, was so named because it gave off "starry," or as the French would say, *astral*, light. It utilized an Argand burner, but the placement of its fuel reservoir reduced the shadows of earlier Argand lamps. Astral lamps were noted for their beautifully shaped etched- and cut-glass shades, which diminished shadows.

**LEFT:** *Although patented before Victoria's reign, the astral lamp became enormously popular during the Victorian period. Today, it is much sought after by collectors.* **RIGHT:** *It was William Morris of England who started the Arts & Crafts Movement; his mission was carried on in the United States by the likes of Gustav Stickley. Ultimately, followers of the movement developed rectilinear furniture forms that bear little resemblance to what is commonly thought of today as Victorian.*

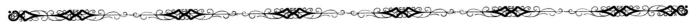

balconies in the upper stories were more common and were made with brackets and railings of wood, cast-iron, wire, or stone. Victorians were aware of the dangers of a child's head getting caught in widely spaced balusters, so they were careful to put the balusters close together. Far cheaper than bay windows, balconies also allowed Victorians to enjoy a wide prospect while waiting for their rooms to cool on summer evenings.

## BALCONIES

Balconies have been restored to Victorian buildings far less frequently than any other exterior feature, even though they were practical as well as decorative devices—especially on the simple wall surfaces of romantic homes in neoclassical styles. The roofs of verandas and bay windows were readily converted to balconies by the installation of a parapet or balustrade above the eaves. Window

## BALCONY GARDENS

According to *Vick's Flower and Vegetable Garden* (1878), "Handsome balconies filled with beautiful, thrifty plants give more pleasure than would thousands of dollars expended in architectural display. More regard must be had to elegant foliage than beautiful flowers." Edward Sprague Rand's *Flowers for the Parlor and Garden* (1864) discusses the practicalities of balcony gardening: the need for adequate watering, since potted plants in semi-open

© Nancy Hill

locations do not fully benefit from rain and tend to dry out; the need for adequate drainage to avoid over-watering; the fact that the only everlasting balcony plantings are evergreens that are protected from direct sunlight, since the combination of daytime thawing and nighttime freezing kills potted plants; "do not plant too much, be content with a few good plants—by trying to grow many you will succeed with none"; and "if your balcony is small, do not attempt to grow shrubs, but be content with climbers for the sides, a few hardy herbaceous plants, and annuals." The balcony garden combined a trellis, potted shrubs, flower boxes, and hanging baskets—all transportable to an interior bay window or conservatory. Rand recommended *Weigela rosea*, climbing cobea, maurandia, nasturtiums, scarlet beans, morning glories, cypress vine, canary bird flower, sweet peas, Madeira vine, loasa, calampelis, physianthus, mignonette, Indian pinks, sweet alyssum, phlox, nemophila, verbena, heliotrope, salvia, larkspur, dielytra, iris, bloodrot, gladiolus, and tiger flower.

# BANDBOXES

Although these round, handmade, decorated wooden boxes were used to store a variety of personal belongings, they usually held hats during the period from the 1820s to the 1850s, when fancy hats were at the peak of their popularity. These boxes were decorated with scraps of leftover wallpaper or with wallpaper made especially for them.

# BANKS

The popularity of neoclassical styles for American "temples of finance" was established in 1797, long before the Victorian period, when the First Bank of the United States was built in Philadelphia with a handsome Georgian portico in the Corinthian order. Frank Furness, an inspired advocate of high Victorian Gothic, persuaded the Provident Life and Trust Company of Philadelphia to build a bank in his personalized version of that style in 1876. It was an eccentric design within the Victorian tradition, despite its fame in twentieth-century architectural history books. The design was good for a bank, because its energized massings of stone masonry and compressed columns conveyed the desirable qualities of strength, stability, and security.

# BASKETS OF FLOWERS

"Considering the effect," wrote Peter Henderson in *Practical Floriculture* (1887), "flowers on the table, like plants in the garden, are certainly the cheapest of ornaments." In retrospect, many fashionable Victorian table decorations were made to look like something else: confections were decorated and arranged to look like flower gardens; baskets of flowers were designed to look like confections. Henderson complained that "table bouquets made in the fashion of the confectioner's stiff pyramids of macaroons are wretched decorations, and very discreditable to all connected with them. Better, a thousand times, to have half the quantity of flowers decently arranged." For table decorations, Henderson recommended either oval or round baskets with or without handles, arranged in either the tight, formal style of the 1860s or the loose, *negligé* style of the 1840s and 1880s.

---

**OPPOSITE PAGE:** *Victorians adored the outdoors, and balconies and balcony gardens were two of the many ways they got closer to nature.*

© Keith Scott Morton

## BATHROOM FURNISHINGS

Washington Irving was one of the first Americans to have indoor plumbing, but it was not in general use during the early Victorian decades. After plumbing technology was perfected in the early 1870s, fashionable homes had bathrooms integrated into their plans. By the 1880s, the catalogs of "art manufacturers" and makers of plumbing products were filled with hundreds of artistic furnishings to beautify late Victorian bathrooms: floor and dado tiles, rugs, wallpapers, fancy lighting devices, elegant cabinetry, and stained glass. Such rooms looked more like baptistries than places for physical relief. Early Victorian bathrooms were sparsely furnished, poorly illuminated, and always

located on a nether corner of the house where leakage might do minimum damage. Early as well as late Victorians encased the new plumbing technology in familiar furniture forms, hence the migration of the footstool, chiffonier, and chest of drawers from the parlor and bedroom to the bathroom.

## BAY WINDOWS

Andrew Jackson Downing, in *Cottage Residences* (1842), showed "A Cottage in the English Rural Gothic Style" with "elegance conferred on the parlor by the bay window, after the old English mode." By 1857, when Calvert Vaux's

*Villas and Cottages* was published, the bay window was a popular feature of Victorian homes in every style. "The *bay-window*," he said, "is the peculiar feature next to the veranda that an American home loves to indulge in. There can scarcely be too many for the comfort of the house, or too few for the comfort of the purse, for I regret to add that they are expensive features." In plan they were either square, rectangular, three- or five-sided "semi-octagon," or circular (a bow window). Occasionally, a bay window would be stacked on a bay window of the same size or slightly larger; sometimes a bay window supported a

🔲 **OPPOSITE PAGE:** *There is nothing more glorious than one of these roomy Victorian claw-foot bathtubs. Most people who were lucky enough to have indoor plumbing kept decoration to a minimum for all manner of health reasons. Wallpaper, for example, was considered unsanitary; tile was preferred. Curiously enough, it was considered chic to leave the pipes exposed. Indeed, one tastemaker advised gilding the plumbing.* **ABOVE:** *A bay window did more than let light in; it provided ample space for elaborate draperies, statues, and, if the house didn't have a conservatory, exotic plants.*

second-floor porch or terminated in a balcony. Vaux offers the following advice for anyone designing a bay window: "a great deal will always depend on the arrangements made for the shutters or blinds; so scanty a space for the piers [is allotted] at the angles, that the shutters are found to be in the way, except when closed, which is, of course, annoying."

## BEAR FURNITURE

Often erroneously called Black Forest furniture, bear furniture was made in Switzerland for those who took the Grand Tour and couldn't bear to leave without a souvenir. Bear furniture is one of the best examples of fantasy furniture: cute carved cubs can be seen climbing up chair legs, holding up benches, and giving bear hugs to chairs. Victorians weren't the only ones who fell in love with this furniture; it was made from the 1880s to the 1950s, and now several pieces are being reproduced.

## BEDDING PLANTS

"As commonly used," wrote Edward Sprague Rand in *Flowers for the Parlor and Garden* (1864), "this term is given to plants which are winter inhabitants of the green-house, but which, if planted in the garden, bloom profusely all summer. They are generally green-house perennials, but among them are included many plants which will bloom late in the summer, from seed sown the same spring, and of which fine varieties are propagated by cuttings." Rand recommended *Ganzia splendens*, verbena, lantana, heliotrope, calceolarias, horseshoe geraniums, petunias, *Cuphea platycentra*, double white feverfew, nierembergia, salvias, *Tritoma uvaria*, carnation and picotee pinks, tea roses, pansies, daisies, ageratum, lychnis, bouvardeas, antirrhinums, gaillardia, lemon verbena, and lobelia.

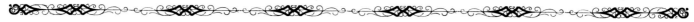

## BED FURNISHINGS

Components of decorating the traditional bed have not varied from the Victorian period to now, with the exception that all fashionable Victorian bedsteads had footboards as well as headboards. Long after Victorian technologies of central heating and flyscreening rendered obsolete the curtained four-poster and the half-tester, or cornona (for the suspension of mosquito nets), these additions survived in late Victorian bedsteads, despite Aesthetic Movement criticism that suggested their simplification. Fashionable bedsteads were draped in the fabrics and style of the bedroom windows. The finest beds, which required hired help as well as expensive fabrics to complete, were elaborately made with embroidered, quilted, or woven coverlets; dust ruffles, pillow shams, and wool flannel sheets for winter use; and linen sheets for summer use. As many of today's Victoriana lovers have discovered to their dismay, purchasing a Victorian bedstead is not half as expensive as filling the linen closet with furnishings for it.

## BEDROOM/NURSERY FURNITURE

Rare illustrations of furniture in Samual Sloan's *Homestead Architecture* (1861) showing Paris designs of the 1840s imply that Victorians furnished bedrooms with "suites" of the same design and material. This was actually the exception. A basic set of "chamber furniture" included a bedstead, wardrobe, bureau, and washstand. Late Victorians resurrected the four-poster bed for Colonial Revival bedrooms, replaced the washstand with a separate bathroom, and substituted closets for wardrobes. Carved, solid rosewood was in the mansion class. Solid walnut with applied carving and veneered mahogany was in the villa class. Painted or grained pine was called "cottage furniture." Bedrooms were nearly always conceived and decorated for a feminine domain, in which light and cheerful colors, pretty patterns, much needlework, and plenty of textiles were in evidence. Late Victorians did away with wall-to-wall carpets and sometimes replaced them with straw matting, on which were arranged one or two rugs. Justified on the grounds that it was unsanitary, wallpaper was replaced with paint; draperies were eliminated for the same reason as much as possible. Perhaps the most progressive achievement was the improvement of children's rooms. "Nothing has struck me as so utterly cruel," wrote Robert Edis in *Decoration and Furniture of Town Houses* (1881), "as the dreariness which generally pervades [children's rooms]. Let the walls be papered with some pleasant paper, in which the color shall be bright and cheerful. There are some charming papers by Mr. Walter Crane, illustrating some of the best-known nursery tales and rhymes."

**OPPOSITE PAGE:** *In general, bedroom furnishings were not quite as fancy as those in the public rooms of the house. The Victorians made quite a distinction between private and public rooms. The bedroom, of course, was the most private, and as such, it was placed on a separate (usually upper) floor of the house.* **ABOVE:** *Small children spent most of their time in the nursery, a separate room that was usually tucked far away from the public rooms. Sometimes, part of the nursery was turned into a schoolroom. Little has been written about decoration of the nursery, but wallpaper designed specifically for children's rooms was first created during Victorian times.*

## BELT COURSES

Late Victorian architects converted the medieval "belt" (a horizontal molding projecting from naked masonry) and the neoclassical string course (a horizontally projecting molding or projecting row of bricks delineating the first story from upper stories) into an ornamented and polychromed belt course, which often defined the transition between different wall coverings. A favorite device found in Queen Anne homes was an oversized belt course expanded to include the sills of second-floor windows and the lintels of first-floor windows.

## BELTER FURNITURE

John Henry Belter (1804–1863) was a German cabinet-maker who emigrated to New York in the 1840s and perfected an efficient method of producing elaborately curved but very strong furniture that was made from laminated sheets of wood. Intricate carving completed his masterful adaptations of Rococo Revival style, which was in vogue during the 1850s. Although it was reviled during much of the twentieth century as the worst example of Victorian furniture, Belter's work is now recognized as the finest furniture of its time.

© Robert Perron

# BENTWOOD FURNITURE

Bending moistened or steamed pieces of wood was not a Victorian technology, but Michael Thonet (1796–1871) mechanized the process for the mass production of furniture. He patented the technique in Vienna in 1842 and made a splendid showing at London's Crystal Palace Exhibition of 1851. Apologists for twentieth-century avantgarde design lauded Thonet's work as a Victorian ancestor of modern furniture, and today's production of bentwood furniture is still sold as such. In the context of his own time, Thonet's exuberant outlines were an expression of the Victorian Rococo Revival style.

# BERLIN WOOL WORK

No variety of Victorian needlework is so characteristic of its time as the early Victorian canvas work called Berlin wool patterns, so named for the German source of many printed patterns sold throughout the Victorian world. Advocates of the late Victorian Aesthetic Movement design philosophy, such as Lady Alford (who wrote *Needlework as Art*, 1886), might say that "the total collapse of our decorative needlework came with the advent of Berlin wool patterns," but they were popular throughout the Victorian period. Copies of famous paintings made by this method were pretentious disasters, but the more decorative patterns, including the ubiquitous recumbent dog resident on a footstool, were delightful components of Victorian chairs, ottomans, fire screens, hand screens, waistcoats, bell-pulls, etc. The colors of Berlin work, both before and after the patenting of aniline dyes by Sir William Perkin in 1856, are phenomenal.

# BIEDERMEIER FURNITURE

Although true Biedermeier furniture was made in Austria and Germany from 1815 to 1830, this simple style, which emphasized light wood, geometric shapes, and flat surfaces, prevailed until 1849. It was given the rather derogatory name Biedermeier—*bieder*, or "plain" in German, and *meier*, a common surname—by the succeeding generation of tastemakers, who considered it way out of style.

# BIRD CAGES

The most famous Victorian song about a bird cage, of course, is the indictment of pretty women who marry for money, called "She's Only a Bird in a Gilded Cage." Fancy bird cages were justified by reasoning that it would insult beautiful birds and their delightful songs to keep them in ugly cages; of course, it would also insult the elegant parlors in which they were kept. Never mind that the birds often made messes on the expensive carpets beneath them—these miniature aviaries were a potent symbol of genteel Victorian living, and countless canaries, parakeets, bullfinches, and goldfinches were incarcerated in these ornamental Victorian prisons.

**OPPOSITE PAGE:** *This Belter bed is typical of the fine craftsmanship associated with the work of John Henry Belter, whose name was so closely linked with Rococo Revival style that much of the furniture in that style came to be called Belter.* **ABOVE, TOP:** *Traces of the Rococo Revival style can be seen in this curvaceous bentwood chair.* **ABOVE:** *Bentwood furniture was often used in cafes because it was inexpensive and (virtually) indestructible. This modern settee by the furniture manufacturer Thonet is part of their Café Daum series.*

**ABOVE:** *Victorians found that the conservatory was the perfect place not only for plants but for an assortment of bird cages and mini aviaries. This mini aviary, with its pagodas and Japonesque stand, would have been in style during the latter part of the century, when the Japanese craze swept the country.* **OPPOSITE PAGE:** *These Victorian aviaries in an English public garden are typically ornate.*

© Nancy Hill

## BIRDHOUSES/AVIARIES/ DOVECOTES

Caged and open dwellings for birds in the garden land-scape were popular Victorian outbuildings and are enjoy-ing a revival. The public aviary, like those on the grounds of Victorian parks like New York City's Central Park, were usually large wire cages, either circular or polygonal, and had a fancy roof shape and cornice trimmings. Birdhouses and dovecotes for Victorian homes were built in cottage, villa, and mansion sizes and ornamented in emulation of various romantic house styles, such as Gothic Revival, Ital-ianate, and Mansardic. In addition to being freestanding in the landscape, they were sometimes attached to the out-side walls of gable peaks of Victorian homes or barns.

## BLOOMERS

By the middle of the nineteenth century, women were get-ting fed up with being trussed up, and several fashion reformers emerged. Although it was named after suffragist Amelia Bloomer, who wholeheartedly endorsed and wore it, the "Bloomer costume," which became the uniform of the women's rights movement from 1851 to 1854, was not designed by her. By our standards, the costume, which consisted of a knee-length skirt and a pair of voluminous trousers gathered at the ankles, isn't worthy of comment, but to the Victorians, it was hysterically comical and a great inspiration for caricature. (Alas, Amelia and the oth-ers abandoned the bloomers, for, of all things, the hoop-skirt.) The term "bloomers," however, was used to refer to that type of trouser and even became a nickname for some types of women's underwear.

## BOARD AND CARD GAMES

Amusements in the nineteenth century were fairly simple. Because transportation was difficult, people stayed at home or at least close to home. Although the Victorians invented few new games—Chinese checkers was one— they did appropriate ones from the past, particularly the eighteenth century. They played by the rules "according to Hoyle," as the expression went; Edmond Hoyle (1672– 1769) was an Englishman who produced the first defin-itive book on the subject. Whist, the Victorian version of contract bridge, solitaire, and even bingo, which was Victorianized to educate young minds about vocabulary, history, literature, and the natural sciences, were all pop-ular pastimes.

Card games, too, were educational; the Montgomery Ward & Co. catalog of 1895 lists several, including Authors, Capital Cities, Mathematiques, Proverbs, and the Wild Flower Game.

The Victorians also played chess, tiddledywinks, dom-inoes, Parcheesi, parlor pool, and the Ouija or Egyptian Luck Board, just to mention a few. (And, yes, there were even those who gambled, but this activity was not referred to in polite company.)

## BOG OAK JEWELRY

An Irish contribution to the array of mourning jewelry that was in vogue after Prince Albert's death, bog oak jewelry was made from the jetlike dark brown wood taken from the peat bogs of Ireland. The Crystal Palace Exhibition of 1851 introduced bog oak to the general public, and it remained popular until about 1885. In fact, crosses were often made of bog oak.

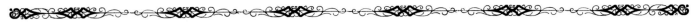

## BOOKS

Unquestionably, the Gilded Age was the golden age of the written word, and the novel in particular. Advances in printing technology made it possible to create inexpensive books, making them widely available to the middle class for the first time. People couldn't wait to read the latest ones. (This interest in reading is truly amazing considering that the quality of the lighting and of the printing were so poor.)

People were eager to read about history, current events, foreign and exotic lands, scientific discoveries, and inventions, and wanted to be able to spout poetry to each other while courting.

The classics, such as Shakespeare's works, continued to be popular at the same time that new authors were appearing. Charles Dickens, who is considered the inventor of the written equivalent of the soap opera, wrote serialized novels, making sure that each installment ended with a cliffhanger that kept people coming back for more. So popular were Dickens' novels that when the last installment of *The Old Curiosity Shop* was shipped to the United States in the 1840s, for example, some four thousand people lined the docks of Boston and begged the captain to tell them whether the heroine, Little Nell, had died.

The American humorist Mark Twain, although not very popular in his own country, was an enormous success in England. Both his novels, like *The Adventures of Tom Sawyer*, and his humorous travel accounts, such as *A Tramp Abroad*, were in great demand.

There were scores of writers on scores and scores of subjects. Bloomingdale's Illustrated 1886 Catalog devotes nearly an entire page to books, including everything from a six-volume set of Washington Irving's works to something called *How to Amuse an Evening Party*. Some of the Victorians' favorite writers included Rudyard Kipling, Edgar Allan Poe, Charlotte and Emily Brontë, and Louisa May Alcott. Poetry by Byron, Browning, Wordsworth, Tennyson, and Coleridge was memorized and recited aloud.

The best way to really understand the period is to read some of the books it produced, which are filled with details of daily life and interior decoration. Even some of the later novelists like Edith Wharton (*House of Mirth*, *The Age of Innocence*) wrote fiction that focused on the manners and mores of the time.

## BORDER BEDS

Victorians used annuals, perennials, and bedding plants in narrow beds bordering walks and paths. Frank J. Scott's *Art of Beautifying Suburban Home Grounds* (1870) describes the "simplest and rudest mode: a continuous bed from two to four feet wide, filled with flowering plants of all sizes and shapes and periods of bloom—overhanging the walk with unkempt growth like weeds." Scott also described today's style of border beds. He and other late Victorian garden designers preferred more formal flower beds "cut into the grass." To embellish straight walks, "they should rarely be cut nearer than two feet from the side of the walk if this length is parallel with it." If openings between circular or square beds with their points to the walk are frequent "one foot of grass will answer….Narrow beds of formal outlines or geometric forms of a simple character, are preferable to irregular ones. All complicated 'curlicue' forms should be avoided." Scott recommended that border beds be "arranged so that a rolling lawnmower may be used easily by hand between them."

## BOULEVARDS AND PROMENADES

Paris was the ideal landscaped city of the Victorian period, especially during the Second Empire, when Napoleon III revived the glories of French Baroque under the direction of Hausmann and Alphand. "Paris exhibits," wrote William Robinson in *Parks, Promenades, and Gardens* (1869),

⊠ *For the first time in history, the printed word became widely accessible to the middle class, and inexpensive magazines, books, and newspapers proliferated. It was the golden age of the novel, with Charles Dickens in England and later Mark Twain in the United States leading the way. Poetry was also quite popular.*

"the noblest and most praiseworthy attempts yet seen to render an originally close and dirty city healthy and pleasant to man; and this has been chiefly effected by her vast system of boulevards—wide well-made open streets and roads bordered with trees, and excellent footways as wide as many of the old streets, or wider." These boulevards were publicized in the most magnificent landscape architecture book of the nineteenth century, Alphand's *Promenades of Paris* (1868). Boulevards did not become fashionable in the United States until late in the nineteenth century, when they appeared in private residential districts and genteel subdivisions. Such walkways are part of what is called the Beaux Arts style of design, because its most prominent practitioners had been trained in Paris at the Ecole des Beaux Arts. Its major impact followed the Columbian Exposition of 1893 in Chicago, laid out by Daniel Burnham. His famous dictum, "Make no little plans," spawned several major boulevards in the early twentieth century, most notably the Benjamin Franklin Parkway linking the Philadelphia Museum of Art and City Hall.

fastening to the lapel. Hand bouquets were larger and more elaborate versions of the buttonhole bouquet, usually arranged in a fan shape around a central flower stemmed to the stick handle, with a decorative covering for the handle and bottom of the bouquet, manufactured and sold as bouquet papers.

© Kent Oppenheimer

## BOUQUETS

According to *Vick's Flower and Vegetable Garden* (1878), "The *Button-hole Bouquet* is composed of a very few fine flowers tastefully arranged. This must not be confounded with the *Button-hole Flower*, which is simply a single flower, like a rosebud, or a tuberose. No leaves are more desirable for this purpose than the sweet-scented Geraniums: Balm, Apple, Dr. Livingston, and Rose." It was fashionable during the late Victorian decades for gentlemen as well as ladies to wear buttonhole bouquets or flowers. The flowers were often "stemmed" with broombrush or wire and moistened by damp moss surrounded by tinfoil. Small arrangements were sometimes placed in a little glass bouquet bolder, with a pin attached to its metal collar for

## BRACKETS

The most popular device for ornamenting the exteriors of Victorian homes was the bracket, which normally appeared as part of an entablature, veranda, or balcony. Twentieth-century designers criticize them as being somehow disingenuous, because they are nonstructural, but Victorians used them to add both beauty and strength to horizontal lines and to soften right angles. Andrew Jackson Downing's *Cottage Residences* (1842) said they were "introduced whenever a support is really or apparently necessary." Despite the efforts of late Victorian architects to eliminate them in what is today called the Stick Style and the Shingle Style, brackets never went out of fashion. Brackets typical of the 1870s were being sold in millwork

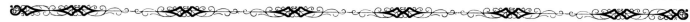

catalogs as late as 1915. They are often painted today in a contrasting color and extensively accented, which tends to make them one-step in isolation instead of waltz in concert with the other elements of the entablature. If it is the case that brackets should be painted the same color as the remainder of the entablature, it is wise, by the same token, to pick them out with a contrasting shade. So, if the brackets appear lost in a dark trim color, make the trim color a little lighter.

## BRASS BEDS

Considered more hygienic because they were easier to clean and were free of the bug infestations that chronically affected wooden beds, brass beds made their appearance in the 1890s. Although cast-iron beds were introduced in the 1850s as substitutes for the more costly wooden styles

of the Rococo Revival and were painted to look like wood, brass beds were considered not only thoroughly modern, but chic. Brass-and-iron beds also were common late in the century. Although these beds are often painted black or white today, they were much more colorful in Victorian times, with reds, greens, and browns being common color recommendations.

## BRIC-A-BRAC

This was a generic Victorian term for any collection of small, decorative items displayed in one of the public rooms of a home. During the Victorian period, as the demand for knickknacks exceeded the supply offered by antiquity and nature, Victorian glass and ceramic manufacturers designed curiously attractive items especially for the bric-a-brac and souvenir trades. The popularity of "art

© Nancy Hill

**OPPOSITE PAGE:** *Brackets are the most prominent feature of Italianate architecture.* **ABOVE:** *Bric-a-brac — what we in this century would call clutter — was considered an integral element in Victorian interiors. But bric-a-brac was not merely an assortment of items set upon a tabletop. It was a collection of objects that had sentimental value, such as a "treasure" that had belonged to a dear departed one or a memento from a Grand Tour abroad.*

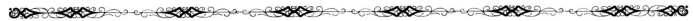

manufacturers" and do-it-yourself "home arts" in the 1870s exacerbated instead of relieved the situation, and a reaction against these trifles began in the 1880s. Louisa Phillips, in an 1888 *Good Housekeeping* article about "A Land of Bric-a-Brac," said "the universal Mrs. Spoopendye placidly proceeds in her art labors, transfixing 'Japanese monsters on Yankee stone jars,' and the universal Mr. Spoopendye continues to fall over them until even masculine human nature can endure it no longer, and one day he turns the whole menagerie out of doors, and once more the house of Spoopendye is a home instead of an amateur museum or old curiosity shop."

# BRIGHTON'S ROYAL PAVILION

This, the most famous bachelor pad of the nineteenth century, was finished long before Victoria's reign, but she and her family spent many pleasant days there. The pavilion was in Brighton, the site of England's first seaside resort. She inherited it from King George IV, who started work on it in 1786 (when it was a farmhouse and he was a randy prince). George not only took a house at Brighton, but also took a secret wife, Maria Fitzherbert, a young Catholic widow. (For the record, he did later take a royal wife, Caroline of Brunswick, but the marriage didn't work and he started a succession of adventures with the wives of various noblemen.)

Over the course of nearly four decades, he transformed the pavilion into an eccentric and exotic palace filled with crystal chandeliers decorated with dragons, palm-tree pillars, faux-bamboo furniture, and all manner of Oriental effects. All in all, the pavilion gave a whole new meaning to the word "eclectic," even in the Victorian context.

# BRILLIANTINE

The city-slicker look was in during the Victorian era, and to achieve it, men applied a liberal amount of brilliantine not only to their hair, but to their mustaches. Montgomery Ward & Co., which carried it in its 1895 catalog for twenty cents per bottle, highly recommended it for "giving a glossy appearance." And, the catalog went on to note, "it is perfectly harmless."

# BRISTOL GLASS

"Bristol glass" is a generic term for Victorian opaque blown glass manufactured in Europe, Bohemia, and the United States, as well as in Bristol, England. It was decorative glass, and late Victorian pieces were especially ornate. Some were designed for the table as finger bowls, rose bowls, and salts. Others were ornate water sets with goblets, tumblers, and water pitcher. But the most popular forms were vases and pairs of cologne bottles for the bedroom dresser or bureau.

© Steve Vidler / Leo de Wys. Inc.

## BUILDING MATERIALS: METAL

Victorian architecture might be divided into old building materials used in new ways and new building materials used in old ways. Victorian inventiveness was most dramatic in the use of metals: cast-iron, steel, and tinplate. The steel I-beam of the Victorian era is still in use today. Cast-iron architectural ornament has enjoyed a recent renaissance. Decorative metal roofing tiles, shingles, ridges, crestings, and siding are still available.

## BULB GARDENS

*Vick's Flower and Vegetable Garden* (1878), a late Victorian planting guide published by a Rochester, New York, nursery owner, notes, "There is a sameness about lawn beds that in time becomes tiresome; we are torn from its masses of bright colors, to the Bulb Garden, and there we find each plant in its own character, standing alone, and doing its best

to secure our admiration. The flowers of this class do not keep in bloom a long time, and therefore are not suited for the lawn; but in a position a little retired, like the border of the lawn or in its rear." Vick's especially recommended the lily, the peony, the gladiolus, and the dahlia.

## BUNGALOWS

"In 1801," according to Philip Davies, "an observer [in Bengal] described the English as living in 'what are really stationary tents which have run aground on low brick platforms. They are "Bungalows," a word I know not how to render unless by a Cottage.'" From the Hindustani word *bangala* developed the English word "bungalow," which meant a one-story cottage with a low roofline extended to create a veranda, which is derived from another Hindustani word. "The bungalow," says Davies, "was adopted as the universal form of colonial housing throughout the Empire—from Rangoon to Adelaide, and from Durban to Toronto."

**OPPOSITE PAGE:** *Brighton Pavilion was considered eccentric even in its own day.* **ABOVE, LEFT:** *New technology and new building materials, including versatile metal alloys, allowed more flexibility in architectural design.* **ABOVE:** *Bulb gardens brought a burst of color, albeit brief, to the Victorian landscape.*

## BUSTLE

The woman who followed fashion by wearing a bustle could hardly hustle, nor would she ever dream of doing so, for that would not be considered genteel. The bustle, a framework of metal, braided wire, and whalebone or crinoline that was fastened to the back of the undergarment at the waist, was the replacement for the hoopskirt. The purpose of the bustle was to expand and support the voluminous drapery of the skirt. And, sometimes, for variety, the bustle was combined with the half-hoopskirt. The bustle not only made it difficult to move, but made it impossible to perform certain elemental movements, such as stooping to sit upon a chair. Indeed, special chairs with wider seats were devised just to accommodate this whim of fashion, which persisted for two decades. As time went on, the bustle got smaller and smaller until it was the size of a petite pillow, and finally disappeared in the 1890s. Ida McKinley, wife of U.S. President McKinley, was one of the first to banish the bustle from her closet. If only she had known about the collapsible-chair undergarment, which fit under the bustle and was fully guaranteed to offer rest and comfort to the fatigued wearer, she might not have been so rash.

## BUTTER MOLDS

Because butter was so perishable, it was quite costly until later in the century, when commercial dairies began operating. Butter that was made on private farms was placed into round wooden molds or prints that produced one-pound cakes. The molds and prints were decorated with carvings that often identified the maker.

**ABOVE:** *The Victorian era ushered in various types of undergarments, including the bustle, that greatly restricted the movements of women. Bustles were heavy and cumbersome, giving a whole new meaning to the phrase "sitting pretty."* **OPPOSITE PAGE:** *Cabbage roses were not confined to the garden. They were also found "growing" on a variety of decorative objects, including china, wallpaper, and carpets.*

New York Public Library

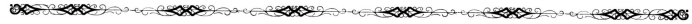

# CALLA LILY

Of all the Aesthetic Movement motifs, the calla lily was most associated with Oscar Wilde, the movement's chief apostle. Not only did he wear this symbol of purity in his lapel, he was often seen walking languidly down to Covent Garden Market with an amaryllis to present to none other than society beauty Lily Langtry. His amorous interest in the woman was apparently quite as pure as the lily, and it has been said that he did it all as a publicity stunt. The image of his beloved calla lily bloomed everywhere on everything from hat pins to curtain tiebacks.

# CALLING CARDS

One of the ways that Victorians kept track of each other was to pay visits or social calls. Calling cards, similar to modern business cards, were the records of these get-togethers. An entire ritual of rules developed around social calls and calling cards. For example, most women kept specific visiting hours during which guests were allowed to call. Each caller left a calling card on the hallway table so that not only the hostess but the other callers could see who had been there. If the hostess was not at home, the caller submitted a card to the servant, turning down one corner to indicate it was delivered in person.

Calling cards were used to announce every important event from wedding receptions to births to deaths. Ten days after a funeral, for instance, it was customary for visitors to leave cards with handwritten messages on them. When survivors were emotionally prepared to receive guests, they sent out black-bordered cards. (As time passed, this border became thinner and thinner until it finally disappeared.)

# CABBAGE ROSES

Victorians were not content to let these sweet-smelling flowers grow only in their gardens. They wanted them indoors all year round, and designers obliged by depicting the large white or pink flowers on everything from wallpapers to carpets. The cabbage rose is not only quintessentially Victorian, it is the stereotypical decoration associated with the period.

# CAMP MEETING GROUNDS

Some of the most fanciful Victorian cottages were built in Methodist camp meeting grounds near large cities. Boston had its Oak Bluffs on Cape Cod, developed in 1866 from the plans of Robert Morris Copeland, and extended in 1880 as Cottage City. New York had its Ocean Grove on the northern New Jersey coast. Beginning as an assortment of tents, many of these sites eventually sported permanent wood-frame buildings on the same small plot that were ornamented with tentlike roofs and tentlike cornice trimmings. A significant portion of tentlike cottage ornamentation in Victorian buildings, especially in seaside resort areas, was derived from the architecture of camp meeting grounds.

# CANOPIES AND HOODS

Calvert Vaux, in *Villas and Cottages* (1857), described the benefits of adding "hoods to windows" as permanent awnings. "The upper sashes of windows with hoods can always be left a little open without any chance of rain beating in; [they defend windows] from the powerful rays of the mid-day sun without shutting it out entirely." The most attractive canopies and hoods have tentlike rooflines and tentlike cornice trimmings.

# CAPITOL BUILDINGS

Over half the buildings still in use as capitols in the United States were designed in the nineteenth century. Many others have been preserved as museums. Of the twenty-eight surviving, only seven had famous architects: Cass Gilbert (Minnesota and Arkansas); Eidlitz and Richardson (New York); Upjohn (Connecticut); Davis (North Carolina); McKim, Mead, and White (Rhode Island); and Strickland

(Tennessee). Ohio's capitol building was adapted from the competition drawings of the famous Hudson River School painter Thomas Cole. Three still in use (Michigan, Texas, Colorado) were designed by the relatively unknown Elijah E. Meyers. In the midst of the Civil War, Thomas U. Walter's cast-iron dome for the capitol in Washington was completed, thereby providing the prototype for nearly all subsequent state capitols.

© MacDonald Photography/Envision

# CARPETS

Victorians had a love/hate relationship with carpets. For most of the nineteenth century, a wall-to-wall carpet or a carpet covering most of the floor was a potent class distinction. Frances Lichten, in *Decorative Arts of Victoria's Era* (1950), documents the social anxiety created between "carpet haves" and "carpet have-nots." During the 1840s in an Ohio pioneer settlement, a lady feared to call on her neighbor because it was rumored she owned a Brussels carpet. It was true, but the neighbor kept it rolled up because she didn't want it destroyed by dirty pioneer feet. Brussels, Wilton, Kidderminster, and Ingrain woven carpets transformed Victorian parlors into chapels of domes-

**OPPOSITE PAGE:** *As the capitol building in Des Moines, Iowa, shows, classical architectural elements gave newly erected state buildings a miraculous injection of instant history.* **ABOVE:** *For most people, wall-to-wall carpeting would have been a luxury. This room successfully combines several Victorian styles of decoration. The étagère and side chairs are Rococo Revival, while the chair in the window is an excellent example of Gothic Revival.*

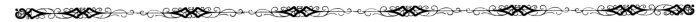

ticity and enforced a reverential social behavior akin to the behavior observed in places of prayer and communion. Victorian carpets, which were florid and gaudy from the beginning, imperiously drove Victorians to the realization that ostentatious interior decoration, especially when a figured and colorful carpet is involved, is monarchical, not democratic. Generally, it was fashionable for early Victorians to have carpets, and expected of late Victorians to avoid them as much as possible (supposedly because an absence of carpeting was more sanitary and alleviated the chore of keeping the floor free from dust). In actuality, late Victorians, particularly those of Aesthetic sensibility who were opposed to carpets, carpeted their walls with densely patterned and richly colored wallpapers that were every bit as unsanitary and flammable.

## CARRIAGE HOUSES/STABLES/ BARNS

The fancier the Victorian house, the more likely its stables or carriage house was built in the same style and with the same materials. Any rectangular box with end gables and a double door will satisfy the basic requirements of a Victorian Revival carriage house. It can be ornamented with board-and-batten siding, central cross-gable, clipped end gables, a ventilator on the roof, and canopies or hoods over the windows. Most barns were painted red because red iron oxides were cheap, readily available, and stable pigments that came in a variety of media from skim milk and lime to linseed oil and white lead. Today's Victorian outbuildings can be painted in personally pleasing colors, as long as they don't conflict with or detract from the house colors. A conservative scheme is to use an intermediate value for the body color of the outbuilding and the trim color of the house for the trim color of the outbuilding.

## CARTES DE VISITE

These visiting cards went one step beyond the calling card; the front side of a carte de visite featured a photograph of the sender. The first ones were homemade, but later, commercial cartes de visite had photographs of celebrities, cities, and landmarks that were taken by the era's foremost photographers. These cards were developed in 1854 when a Frenchman discovered a way to place eight images on one negative. After printing, the images were cut out and glued to cards. So popular did cartes de visite become that people collected whole sets of them and pasted them in albums made specifically for that purpose.

© Lynn Karlin

**ABOVE:** *Yesterday's carriage houses are today's carports and condos. High-style Victorian houses and their carriage houses usually matched, right down to the gingerbread on the gables. In more rural areas, particularly in the wild West, the carriage house would have been called a barn or stable and would have looked strictly utilitarian.* **OPPOSITE PAGE, LEFT:** *For ease of movement, Victorian furniture was on casters, or miniature wheels.* **OPPOSITE PAGE, RIGHT:** *The caryatid was one of the primary features of Renaissance Revival furniture.*

# CARYATID

A caryatid is a female head on a pillar that acts as a support column for a piece of furniture. The Victorians borrowed the style from the late seventeenth century, and used the motif, as well as other versions of the female form, on some of their Renaissance Revival pieces.

# CASTERS

Much Victorian furniture—sofas, dining tables, and parlor tables—was built on miniature wheels made of wood, metal, or porcelain called casters. These wheels not only gave the pieces height, they made the furniture mobile. Although some early pieces of furniture had big brass casters, most of the first casters were wooden. Porcelain ones were popular from about 1860 until the turn of the century. The term also refers to the elaborate sterling or silverplate containers for the dining table, which held everything from salt and pepper to vinegar and oil.

Courtesy of Stingray Hornsby Antiques

# CASTLES

Lacking royalty and a hereditary aristocracy, Americans will say there are no castles in the United States, Victorian or otherwise. Yet many country estates overlooking the Hudson River, Long Island Sound, and other prominent bodies of water qualify on the basis of splendor alone. The most famous "castle" is Lyndhurst (begun in 1838 and completed in 1864–1865), by A. J. Davis in the Gothic Revival style in Tarrytown, New York. The most popular Victorian form of "castle" was the resort hotel. In addition to a fascination with their own "rich and famous," Americans shared with Victorians elsewhere in the world a fascination with European castles—especially those of Queen Victoria and Prince Albert, with Balmoral heading the list. The most famous Victorian "literary castle" was Sir Walter Scott's Abbotsford.

# CEILING DECORATION

Victorians were generally more concerned about how to decorate their ceilings than they were about the walls or any other interior aspect. For the first half of the nineteenth century, the ceiling and cornices were the domain of the decorative plasterer, who supplied centerpieces sometimes called "flowers," moldings for panel and border effects, and the cornices. The most expensive ceilings were sometimes embellished by a decorative painter in addition to the decorative plasterer, and on rare occasions by an artist in stained glass. During the second half of the nineteenth century, ceilings were declared open territory for paperhangers, ordinary painters, and stencilers. There was much discussion about colors, but it was generally agreed that ceilings, because they are highest in the room and therefore most closely related to the sky, should be decorated in lighter colors than those of the walls or the floors.

# CEILING DESIGN

Victorians, no matter how devoted some of them were to pure design, generally agreed that ceilings should echo—sometimes softly and sometimes loudly—the dominant style of the room. Although it was important to more Victorians to have a carpet on the floor than a design on the ceiling, it was even more impressive to have both. The neoclassical approach, which was fashionable during the early nineteenth century, emphasized monochromatic bas-relief sculpture effects made on-site by a decorative plasterer or bought ready-made from a catalog. The historic references were Greek, Roman, Italian Renaissance, French Baroque, and Rococo. During the late nineteenth century, the Aesthetic Movement attempted a fresh

© Dick Dietrich

**OPPOSITE PAGE:** *In Victorian interior design, every surface, even the ceiling, was a decorative canvas. In the most ornate homes, ceilings were hand-stenciled in gold and silver, or displayed scenes painted by well-known artists. In less spectacular homes, a similar effect was achieved with wallpaper specifically designed for the ceiling.* **ABOVE:** *Extensive ceiling decoration expanded the perceived height of the room and made it possible to have a totally integrated interior. Fluffy clouds were often painted upon a light blue background to give the effect of the sky or the heavens.*

approach to ceiling design by experimenting with Oriental motifs and color theory. Perhaps the most interesting aspect of late Victorian ceiling design was the attempt to blend the tops of the walls with the edges of the ceiling by extending richly molded cornices well into the ceilings and linking them with harmonious bands of color. The field of the ceiling was either decorated freehand by a fresco painter on plaster or by a decorative painter on canvas, or it was covered with a suitably "artistic" wallpaper. During the 1880s, neoclassicism returned in the form of Adamesque ceilings of bas-relief ornaments that provided an elegant antidote to these complex cornices, involved color schemes, and highly figured ceilings of the Aesthetic Movement. At a lower level in the social scale of interior decoration, stencil decorations provided art as well as simplicity without expense and anxiety.

## CEILING PAPERS

There was absolutely nothing worse than a white ceiling, or so the Victorians believed. There were several ways to decorate ceiling space, including stenciling, painting decorative murals, and applying ornaments made of wood, plaster of Paris, or papier mâché, but the cheapest way was with paper. From the 1870s to the 1890s, special ceiling paper, which is different from wallpaper, was produced. Tastemakers suggested that ceiling-paper patterns should appear the same from all directions and that the design should be stylized rather than realistic. Ceiling paper was considered a modern treatment, and it was highly recommended because it could be both applied and cleaned easily.

## CEMETERIES

Rural cemeteries, which Victorians often referred to as Cities of the Dead, were prototypes for both the landscaped subdivisions of residential areas and for public parks such as Central Park in New York City. Although these cemeteries are miniaturized museums of Victorian architectural styles, wonderful collections of Victorian sculpture, and repositories of Victorian wrought and cast-iron, their chief glory is the delightful array of Victorian plant material. The best in the United States is also the first landscaped cemetery, Mount Auburn (1831), near Boston at Cambridge, which had formative links with the Massachusetts Horticultural Society.

© Grace Davies / Envision

▦ **ABOVE:** *Before the advent of public parks, the only open spaces in cities were cemeteries. Paying respects to the dead was a family affair: mama, papa, and the children all dressed in their Sunday best and, picnic baskets in hand, spent the day walking among the tombs.* **OPPOSITE PAGE:** *The center table was so named because it was placed in the center of the room and was often the center of attention. Many center tables, such as this one in the Rococo Revival style, had marble tops.*

# CENTER TABLE

The center table not only stood in the center of the parlor, it stood in the center of family life. In well-appointed parlors, it was a small, elaborately carved table, usually round, that often had a marble top. In houses of modest means, where the functions of several rooms were combined, the center table was not quite so fancy and served a variety of uses. Catherine E. Beecher and Harriet Beecher Stowe, in their *American Woman's Home* (1869), advise against spending too much money on one and instead suggest taking a cheap pine table and covering it with green broadcloth trimmed with a border so "that a family of five or six may all sit and work, or read, or write around it, and it is capable of entertaining a generous allowance of books and knickknacks."

# CERAMICS (HAND-PAINTED)

Prior to the development of transfer printing in the early nineteenth century, all ceramics were decorated by hand. "Hand-painting" in the Victorian context refers to a form of art pottery decoration promoted largely for the pleasure and profit of women as part of the Aesthetic Movement of the 1870s. The center for it was in Cincinnati, under the direction of M. Louise McLaughlin, whose *China Painting* (1877) was kept in print well into the twentieth century. From then until now, china painting may have ebbed and flowed with changes in taste, but as any visit to a craft shop today will reveal, this is a Victorian art that is alive and well.

© Mark E. Gibson

# CERAMICS (TRANSFER-PRINTED)

One of the chief beneficiaries of the early-nineteenth-century invention of lithography, a method of printing from a planed surface made of stone or metal, was the Victorian pottery industry. Images on transfer-printed ceramics were cheaply transferred from stone to paper and transferred again to pottery. Because the images on paper were flexible, they could be transferred to curved as well as flat areas. The result was that people could decorate pottery at prices they could afford. The favorite pattern was willow, designed by Thomas Minton in the late eighteenth century; it was romanticized by the addition of tragic lovers into the pattern. The Spode potteries specialized in the pattern during the Victorian period. It has been produced by various potteries throughout the twentieth century, which makes it one of the most accessible forms of Victoriana. Since the early twentieth century, the most popular Victorian transfer-printed collectibles have been those associated with Staffordshire, especially the blue-and-white wares with pictures of places (called "historical blue") and the pictorial lids of food and cosmetic jars that Victorians kept as bric-a-brac.

# CHAIR RAILS

Considered old-fashioned by the early Victorian era, the chair rail, a strip of wood attached to the wall to prevent the backs of chairs from nicking the wall, was resurrected by the mid-nineteenth century, as wall decorations became more elaborate and more costly. As Charles Locke Eastlake argued so persuasively in *Hints on Household Taste* (1872), "I have seen narrow strips of wood nailed down to the floor within an inch or two of the wall. The legs of chairs (and consequently their back-rails) are thus kept off from the paper behind them, and a 'grazing line' is avoided."

# CHAISE LONGUE

Like some other popular Victorian furniture forms, the chaise longue was descended from a late-eighteenth-century form of the same name. Derived from the old sofa and daybed, the chaise longue was used by many Victorians in parlors as an invalid's couch and as the famous "fainting couch" for tightly corseted women when they were momentarily asphyxiated by food or excitement. Because it was a generic term for any long seat used for lounging, it was eventually corrupted into "chaise lounge."

© Edward Addeo

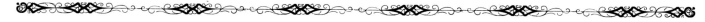

© Kent Oppenheimer

# CHAMBER SETS

Throughout the nineteenth century, most people lacked indoor plumbing, and so the chamber set was a necessity as well as a decorative item in the majority of Victorian bedrooms. A set of this pottery included a pitcher, washbowl, soap dish, shaving mug, toothbrush holder, and the infamous chamber pot. These sets were made in the complete range of popular pottery wares, including stoneware, ironstone, rockingham, and transfer-printed earthenware. Many of them survive in sets or singles, although they are rarely used for their original purpose. In revived Victorian bedrooms one rarely sees that most sensitive addition to the delicate operation of a chamber pot in the middle of the night, the crocheted lid silencer.

**OPPOSITE PAGE:** *Transfer-printed ceramics, based on newfangled technology, found a following among the middle classes, chiefly because they were inexpensive.* **ABOVE:** *The chaise longue, or fainting couch, was not decorative: Victorian women, who were often all trussed up in corsets, really did faint quite a lot. Later, when the Turkish style was all the rage, the form found a place in the parlor, a public room, where it was considered decadent because it allowed the option of reclining in mixed company.* **LEFT:** *Before indoor plumbing, most bedrooms had a washstand that had a pitcher and bowl for washing. Usually made of china and highly decorative, washstands matched the prevailing style.*

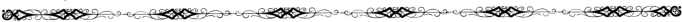

# CHATEAU STYLES

Late Victorians in the United States might have been reluctant to build castles, but they gave architectural expression to the principle that "a man's home is his castle" by utilizing the ornamental features of medieval French chateaux in the Loire Valley. The ultimate American chateau was Biltmore (1895) at Asheville, North Carolina, designed by the Beaux Arts–trained architect Richard Morris Hunt. The lowest common denominator in any chateau-style building was a small tower called a turret. The highest concentration of chateau styles will be found in late Victorian neighborhoods designed for urban gentry of the United States.

**BELOW:** *The nouveaux riches translated the principle "a man's home is his castle" into concrete and stone by building chateaux-style mansions, such as this one in Newport, Rhode Island. Newport became one of the summer playgrounds of the rich and famous.* **OPPOSITE PAGE:** *Architects paid great attention to detail; even chimneys and chimney pots were ornate.*

## CHATELAINE AND CHATELAINE PURSE

Originally referring to the keeper of the keys or the mistress of the chateau, the term "chatelaine" came in the nineteenth century to mean the ornamental clasp that contained the purse, keys, sewing equipment, pen, and other small objects that were needed to run the household. This eventually became the chatelaine purse, a bag suspended from a chain that had a ring that hooked to the waist. The chatelaine purse was usually round, but there were oblong, square, and oval versions. It could be made of beads, wire mesh, or even leather. The ones shown in the Montgomery & Ward Co. catalog of 1895 and one example in Bloomingdale's Illustrated 1886 Catalog are made of leather.

## CHESTERFIELD

The family name of a nineteenth-century Earl of Chesterfield is perpetuated in a thoroughly upholstered, buttoned-and-tufted, double-ended couch of elephantine proportions. It was fashionable in the 1880s and is still being made today, usually in leather. It was considered a man's couch.

## CHIFFONIER

"Chiffonier" is a furniture term that was used to describe a variety of pieces throughout the nineteenth century. During the Regency and early Victorian periods, it was a small casepiece with two hinged doors in the base, surmounted by a shelved backboard, and paired in parlors or dining rooms to flank a fireplace. By the late nineteenth century it had migrated upstairs to the bedroom as a slim chest of drawers.

© Kenneth Martin / Amstock

## CHIMNEYS/CHIMNEY POTS

"The very first things that catch the eye, and the last to escape observation," said Calvert Vaux in *Villas and Cottages* (1857), are chimneys. "They should always seem to stride the ridge, and never appear to sit on it side-saddle fashion, for a very disagreeable monotony of line will be the result." Vaux despised clay chimney pots, calling them "the most mean, shabby, dwarfish features that can be added to a house." These manufactured devices were popular because they provided an ornamented chimney without the expense of handcraftsmanship. Chimney pots are still available in a limited number of Victorian designs. Late Victorian homes often had the chimneys exposed far down on the roofs. This required tall stacks, which were ornamented with patterned brickwork, recessed panels, corbeled caps, and terra-cotta inserts. Another popular late Victorian treatment was to fully expose the chimneys on the outside wall from ground level to cap.

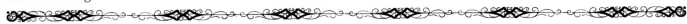

# CHINA PAINTING

Although it attracted a lot of amateur painters, china painting was one hobby that at least some Victorian women were able to turn into a profession. Next to needlework, it was the most popular craft. It was also one of the few fields in which it was considered proper for women not only to work but to achieve a bit of success. Interest in china painting led to the establishment of ceramics studios and ceramics societies.

# CHRISTMAS CARDS

Although Sir Henry Cole of England commissioned John Calcott Horsley to illustrate the first Christmas card in 1843, the rest of the public had to wait for better postal service and the invention of cheap color printing before they were able to send "season's greetings." Cole's card, of which about one thousand copies were made so he could send them to his closest friends, depicted several Dickensian figures making merry and helping the needy, and had this simple message: "Merry Christmas and Happy New Year to You."

Because manufacturers, who had had a tremendous success with valentines (the first mass-produced greeting cards), didn't want to alter a winning formula, their first yuletide cards, complete with arrow-bearing Cupids, tended to wax poetic with love poems and posies.

By the 1870s, the printer Louis Prang of Boston was the most popular Christmas-card maker in the United States. Although his first cards were simply calling cards with holiday messages, later ones became larger and more lavish.

# CHRISTMAS GIFTS

Christmas was definitely a time of giving, but not in the least like it is today. Presents were meant to be personal, rather practical, and homemade. Pincushions, sachets, shaving-paper cases, decorated calendars, frames, collar cases, hair receivers, and pen wipers were just some of the items that were deemed suitable for giving.

# CHRISTMAS TREE

Although Prince Albert did not bring the tradition of the Christmas tree to Windsor, he did popularize it. The first Christmas trees were small enough to fit on the top of parlor tables and were decorated not with ornaments, but with candles and the gifts the family was giving to each other. (Prime examples of such presents included oranges and tiny baskets of chocolates and other sweets, which were expensive delicacies at the time.) Later trees were larger, and some, like the ones in Queen Victoria's palace, were hung from the ceilings in place of chandeliers. (It should be noted that nobody has yet discovered whether Victoria had them suspended upside down or right-side up.)

What Prince Albert did not do by way of establishing Christmas customs, Charles Dickens did. *A Christmas Carol*, Scrooge and all, recorded in great detail exactly how Victorian England celebrated the holiday in the 1840s, right down to the parlor games and turkey dinners.

**OPPOSITE PAGE:** *This illustration for a Christmas card won first prize in one of Louis Prang's design competitions.* **ABOVE:** *The first Christmas trees were placed atop parlor tables and were decorated with sweets and fruits, which, before mass transportation made such perishables widely available, were expensive delicacies. Hand-blown glass ornaments were introduced later in the century.*

Palubniak Picture Archive

## CHROMOLITHOGRAPHY

By the late nineteenth century, those who wanted exposure to great art at little cost could hang chromolithographs, or chromos, in their homes. These cheap color copies of classic paintings, which were sometimes varnished before being hung in elaborate frames, were made possible through an improvement in lithography that allowed mass production by eliminating hand tinting. Although chromos were the darling of the middle class from about 1860 to 1900 and although they were championed by Catherine E. Beecher and her sister Harriet Beecher Stowe in their landmark *American Woman's Home* (1869), many people of means considered them vulgar and garish.

## CIGAR LIGHTERS

From about the mid-nineteenth century, in the days of gaslight, cigar lighters looked a lot like little figural lamps. They were about six to fourteen inches tall and came in a variety of masculine motifs. The Mitchell, Vance & Co. catalog, circa 1876, has several examples in various shapes, including a stag, a dog, a horse, a sailor, and even a fire hydrant.

## CITY HALLS/TOWN HALLS

The architecture of Victorian cities, which were often enlarged by the annexation of smaller surrounding cities, commonly made reference to the colonnades of ancient Athens, the arcades of ancient Rome, the towers of Renaissance Italy and northern Europe, or the Mansardic rooflines of Haussman's rebuilding of Paris (1852–1870) for Napoleon III. Town and city walls in particular reflected the styles of the past. Philadelphia City Hall, designed by John McArthur, Jr., in the Mansardic style and begun in 1871 for completion by 1876 for the Centennial, was not finished until 1904, thereby enriching two generations of politicians and contractors. Other surviving Mansardic city halls are in Boston (1862), Baltimore (1867), Norwich (1870), and Providence (1874). Earlier surviving examples in neoclassical style are in Brooklyn (1845), New Orleans (1845), Norfolk (1847), Wilmington, North Carolina (1855), and Petersburg, Virginia (1856). Later surviving examples in Romanesque Revival style are in Albany (1881), Cincinnati (1883), Cambridge (1889), Syracuse (1889), Minneapolis (1889), Lowell (1890), and Salt Lake City (1892). The most famous surviving English town hall is Manchester Town Hall (1868), designed by Alfred Waterhouse. An excellent example of the neoclassical style is Leeds Town Hall (1853), designed by Cuthbert Brodrick.

## CLASSICAL REVIVAL ARCHITECTURE

"Classical Revival" is the delicate phrase used today to overcome the common American prejudice against Greek Revival as "not Victorian," so completely has Andrew Jackson Downing's propaganda of the 1840s against Greek Revival been accepted as dogma. Greek Revival architecture began in the United States in 1800 and was the first national style, but it survived well into Victoria's reign, which began in 1837. Evidence of its enduring popularity is the appearance, two years after Downing's death, of the last edition of Asher Benjamin's Greek Revival builder's guide titled *The Architect, or Practical House Carpenter* (1854). Many prime examples of the style that still survive were built in the 1840s and 1850s. During the 1850s and 1860s, Greek classical revival was modified into Italianate classical revival.

## CLIMBING PLANTS

"The Climbers furnish us with nature's drapery," said *Vick's Flower and Vegetable Garden* (1878). "These tender Climbers surpass all the productions of the decorator's skill.... The strong-growing varieties cover fences, arbors and buildings, and give both grace and shade. Those of more delicate growth are invaluable for posts, baskets, and other decorative purposes." Vick's recommended the following annuals: calampelis, coboea, cardiospermum, convolvulus (morning glory), dolichos (cypress vine), loasa, maurandya, flowering peas, thunbergia, tropaeolum (canary flower). Vick's also recommended the following perennials: *Adlumia cirrhosa* (Allegheny vine), akebia, ampelopsis (Virginia creeper), aristolochia (Dutchman's pipe), celastrus (climbing bittersweet), clematis, hedera (English ivy), lonicera (climbing honeysuckle), Madeira vine, tecoma (trumpet flower), and wisteria.

© Nancy Hill

**OPPOSITE PAGE:** *Chromolithographs, or "chromos" as they came to be called, often depicted sentimental subjects and were, for the most part, considered to be in questionable taste.* **ABOVE:** *Outside, climbing plants were trained to grow across doorways and archways; inside, they were often used to form a naturalistic window curtain. Here, the climbers outside complement the fabric curtains on the inside of the door beautifully.*

© Robert Perron

# COBBLESTONE BUILDINGS

Cobblestone buildings appeared in all early Victorian styles and shapes and were concentrated near local supplies of glacially abraded and lake-washed stones, especially in upstate New York near Rochester. The technique of embedding rows of stone with similar or different shapes in mortar to cover coarse, rubble masonry walls was an old, vernacular European tradition. It was popular in rural areas because it ornamented a masonry structure without the expense and skilled labor required to use cut stone or manufactured brick. Cobblestone facings made it possible for many farmers and artisans to build their own stone homes.

# COLLEGES/UNIVERSITIES

Victorian campuses in the United States were often located in rural areas on the romanticized model of Britain's Oxford and Cambridge, although Victorianized medieval styles derived from them were not used until the end of the nineteenth century, when Collegiate Gothic and College Tudor became the vogue. The most influential campus of the early nineteenth century was Thomas Jefferson's neoclassical "academical village" for the University of Virginia (1817–1826) at Charlottesville, designed as a tangible textbook of the classical orders. Subsequent campuses in the United States were dominated by Victorian forms of neoclassicism, including Mansardic; Ruskinian Gothic and Richardsonian Romanesque sometimes made brave appearances. The most important Victorian stimulus to the architecture of higher education in the United States was the passage of Justin Smith Morrill's Land Grant Act (1862), which established a system of state universities.

© James Blank/FPG International

**OPPOSITE PAGE:** *Cobblestones were sometimes used in the construction of cottages and garden pathways. Here, the leaded windows give an old-fashioned European look to the house.* **ABOVE:** *The high-style architecture of the University of Syracuse in New York was fairly typical of Victorian institutions of higher learning.* **RIGHT:** *The spinning wheel was the most ubiquitous symbol of Colonial Revival furniture. Parts of spinning wheels often found a second life as the backs and seats of chairs. Although such creations were considered innovative and stylish in their day, today they look bizarre.*

## COLONIAL REVIVAL

The Centennial Exhibition held in Philadelphia in 1876 made the Victorians long for the good old days—the days when the Thirteen Colonies revolted against England and became the United States of America. As a result of the exhibition, antiques were suddenly "in." People who couldn't honestly say "George Washington slept here" about their homes began searching their attics for spinning wheels, tall-case clocks, and other Revolution relics. In truly eclectic fashion, they put them next to their Rococo Revival settees and Empire parlor tables. A walk through any furniture store today shows that the Colonial style is still in revival.

## COLONIAL REVIVAL FURNITURE

Those who couldn't find genuine Colonial Revival pieces turned to craftsmen like Wallace Nutting and firms like New York's Sypher & Co. for copies of Colonial Revival furniture. Other companies, however, couldn't resist the temptation to tinker and gave Colonial Revival a revolutionary twist by "improving" and adapting designs. Suddenly, the most staid pieces sprouted curlicues in the strangest places. Perhaps the most original—and most outlandish—adaptation was the spinning-wheel chair. Old spinning wheels became the backs and seats for chairs, and the wheel's legs became the arms of the new creation. In addition, there were spinning-wheel tables, whatnots, hall trees, hat racks, chandeliers, and even settees.

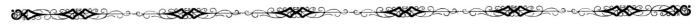

# COMMEMORATIVE MONUMENTS

The model for most Victorian commemorative monuments, also called shrines and memorials, was the ancient Roman Forum, especially Trajan's Column and the Arch of Titus. The famous baroque fountains of Rome were the conceptual basis for many Victorian commemorative fountains. The first important monument of the nineteenth century in the United States was the Washington Monument (circa 1814) in Baltimore by Robert Mills, which was followed by Mills' Washington Monument (conceived in 1833, begun in 1848, and completed, after many financial setbacks, in 1884) in Washington, D.C. The world's most famous Victorian monument in the Gothic Revival style is Edinburgh's Sir Walter Scott Monument.

© Charles Friend

# CONCERT HALLS/OPERA HOUSES/ THEATERS

In their internal arrangements, Victorian entertainment palaces differed little from the horseshoe design perfected in seventeenth-century Italy, although Wagner's Festspielhaus (1876) in Bayreuth, Germany, was an innovation that looked forward to twentieth-century theater designs. For most U.S. cities, a concert hall or opera house, which often doubled as a theater, was a Victorian architectural badge of cultural honor. The world's most famous Victorian entertainment palace was the Paris Opera (circa 1870), designed by Charles Garnier.

# CONSERVATORIES

Edward Sprague Rand's *Flowers for the Parlor and Garden* (1864) warns that a "conservatory" is not a "Stove, Hot-house, or Green-house"; it "is used properly to designate a show house, where the temperature ranges from forty to sixty degrees, and into which plants are removed, when coming into bloom, from the other houses. It is improperly applied to any glass structure in which plants and flowers are grown." "Private conservatories are made for enjoyment," said *Vick's Flower and Vegetable Garden* (1878), "and should be arranged somewhat in the manner of a garden, with a few large and beautiful plants and broad walks. What a blessing a rich man would be to a neighborhood, if he were to build such a conservatory and say to his neighbors and their children that it was constructed partly for their pleasure, and two or three days in a week all were invited to call and enjoy its beauties at their convenience. The idea that people will wilfully injure or destroy plants or flowers is entirely fallacious. If we wished to give an object lesson on good manners, we would point to the gardens where the masses of people congregate. The love of flowers conduces to good deportment."

## COOK, CLARENCE

Aesthetic Movement art critic Clarence Cook (1828–1900) is remembered mostly for books on interior design, including *The House Beautiful* (1881) and *What Shall We Do With Our Walls?* (1884).

## CORNER BOARDS/ PILASTER CORNERS

Practical devices that facilitate the installation of wood siding, corner boards and pilaster corners are ignored or underemphasized in many exterior decoration schemes today, even those polychromed Victorian buildings called painted ladies. In general, superior exterior decoration is based on a firm grasp of architectural functions. Thus, recognizing corner boards and pilaster corners as boundary markers and emphasizing them by appropriate colors often makes the difference between a haphazardly arranged collection of colors, which weakens a building's architectural potential, and a functionally arranged set of colors, which maximizes architectural potential.

**OPPOSITE PAGE:** *Victorians went to great lengths to commemorate not only places and events but people. Most of these monuments took their cue from the Albert Memorial in London, which was Queen Victoria's tribute to her dear departed Albert, from whose untimely death she never recovered.* **ABOVE:** *A new interest in horticulture led to the inclusion of conservatories in upper-class homes; because they were filled with a variety of exotic plants, many resembled glass-enclosed mini jungles. Some even featured fountains and statuary.* **RIGHT:** *Every part of the Victorian home was designed to sport a polychromatic color scheme. One of the major mistakes of today's owners of Victorian homes is to paint all these architectural details the same color, instead of defining them in different hues.*

## CORNICE DRAPERY

"Cornice drapery" is an inclusive phrase for verge boards, peak ornaments, and eave ornaments appearing in late Victorian millwork catalogs. Calvert Vaux called them "roof trimmings" in *Villas and Cottages* (1857), and they reveal the migration of Victorian interior decoration to the exterior of the house. Much of the so-called gingerbread appearing on gables, eaves, and verandas duplicates the tassels, ball fringes, elaborate cornices, and wooden grills of Victorian parlors. This concept is useful in sorting out the functions of Victorian exterior architectural details and selecting colors for them. Many of the fret-sawn ornaments imitate lace panels set within architectural frames, and they can be colored accordingly.

## CORSETS

To achieve a wasp waist, Victorian women laced themselves up in corsets, which were highly fashionable, and highly injurious to the health. The bone and steel stays cut into the flesh, compressing waists to only twelve to fifteen inches, which made it difficult enough to breathe, let alone eat, walk, or dance. In *American Woman's Home* (1869), Catherine E. Beecher and sister Harriet Beecher Stowe detailed the evils of the garment—everything from heart to

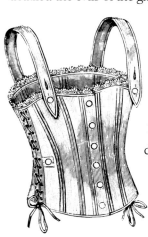

liver problems—and recommended their own revolutionary creation, a corsetlike jacket that offered support without stays. Still, old habits die hard, and in 1886 Bloomingdale's catalog still devoted nearly three pages to the contraptions.

## COTTAGE STYLE ARCHITECTURE

The roots of Victorian cottage styles are found in the early-eighteenth-century Whig liberalism of Britain's Lord Burlington and his circle. Burlingtonians succeeded in changing the British countryside by their advocacy of scientific farming, landscaping of estate grounds in the "natural style," and beautified dwellings for "cottagers," which also featured more humane living conditions. These cottages were rendered more elegant by a bit of French, hence the pleasant term *cottage orné*. In 1842, Andrew Jackson Downing's *Cottage Residences* perverted the original concept of the cottage orné into a pretentious collection of two-story houses. The styles of these stone or wood houses were cottages in English or Rural Gothic, Italian or Tuscan, Old English, Pointed or Tudor, and Bracketed Mode; and villas in the Elizabethan, Italian, and Pointed styles—all of which were offered by Downing as his antidote to what he called America's "blind passion for Grecian temples." *Village and Farm Cottages* (1856), by Cleaveland and Baccus, was closer in spirit to the tradition of the cottage orné in its unpretentious collection of designs arranged as cottages of one story, one story and attic, hillside cottages, houses of two stories, farmhouses, and double cottages. Its target audience was "mechanics and tradesmen of moderate circumstances, the small farmer, and the laboring man." Its goal was "to provide the villager of limited means with a plan for his small house, in which strict economy shall be combined with comfort, good looks, and substantial value."

**OPPOSITE PAGE:** *Cornice drapery, also called gingerbread, was used to fancy up an otherwise ordinary exterior. In this example, three styles of gingerbread frame a Gothic Revival cottage-style house.* **ABOVE:** *Corsets kept waistlines looking thin—and women from breathing. Once the health hazards associated with this garment became common knowledge, reformers called for their abolishment.*

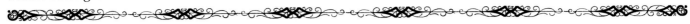

# COTTON BATTING CHRISTMAS ORNAMENTS

Charming and inexpensive, German cotton batting ornaments were made by gluing thin layers of cotton batting
over a wire or cardboard frame. Fruits and vegetables were
popular motifs, as were Santas and angels, which were
decorated with glued-on paper faces. Each ornament was
sprinkled with sparkles, particles of either ground glass or
mica. These decorative figures look like they've just come
in from the snow.

# COUNTRY SCHOOLS

Although one thirty-sixth of federal lands was allocated to
support public education by Thomas Jefferson's North-
west Ordinance of 1787, the United States didn't get serious about public education until 1837, when Horace
Mann, the "Father of the American Public School System,"
became the first secretary of the Massachusetts Board of
Education. Henry Barnard, who became the first commis-
sioner of the U.S. Bureau of Education in 1867, compiled
four books on school architecture from 1842 to 1870. The
one-room schoolhouse, often painted red (hence the term
"the little red schoolhouse") because red oxide paint was
cheap and durable, was often modeled after a Victorian
cottage. Many have since been converted into homes or
offices, and many others are still used as schools by rural
Amish and Mennonite communities.

# COURTHOUSES

Democracy elevated the architecture of courthouses in the
United States to the first rank in those communities that,
by hook or crookedness, managed to get themselves certi-
fied as the county seat or shire town. In most instances,

these courthouses were designed as diminutive capitol
buildings and followed the same trends of Victorian neoclassicism until the completion of H.H. Richardson's
Romanesque Revival Allegheny County Court House in
Pittsburgh in 1888, which was echoed in the Minneapolis
City Hall and Courthouse (1889–1905), designed by Long
and Kees. The most prolific architect of Victorian courthouses was Elijah E. Myers, who designed over one hundred of them.

*James Blank/FPG International*

**ABOVE:** *Courthouses such as this one in Lexington, Kentucky,
were not only halls of justice, but monumental architectural
extravaganzas.* **OPPOSITE PAGE:** *Walter Crane, illustrator extraor-
dinaire, elevated book design to an art. He was also known for
the fanciful nursery wallpapers he designed.*

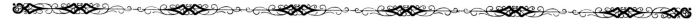

## COURTING

As more than one young man found, courting in the Victorian era was a delicate proposition that required not only discretion but great restraint. Because nothing was spelled out and these matters were not often discussed candidly, sometimes accidents did happen. For example, it is said that the Englishman Edward Heneage Dering, a superlative Catholic gentleman, ended up marrying Lady Chatterton, a noted novelist, because when he went to ask for the hand of her niece, the painter Rebecca Dulcibella Orpen, the good lady misunderstood and thought he was proposing to her. Although Rebecca and Edward finally wed in 1884, they had had to wait for nearly two decades, until their spouses died.

Not everyone found courting so disconcerting as Edward Dering, but many found it difficult even to meet members of the opposite sex, and once they were introduced—always by a friend or relative—they were not really allowed to get to know much about each other before wedding bells started ringing. A good girl—and during Victorian times most of them had to be—never went out alone with a man at night, and even during the day a young woman had to get her mother's permission just to be with a man.

When he did finally pop the question, the girl was advised to be coy even if she adored him. She was not to reveal her true feelings, and, so as not to appear too eager, she often said no the first time. (Queen Victoria, however, because of her station in life, was actually required to propose to Albert, who not only had been groomed for her but had been eagerly waiting for her to do so.) If a young woman said yes, it was then that the young man, with great trepidation, asked her father for her hand.

## COZY CORNER

The most romantic form of late Victorian inglenookery was the Turkish cozy corner. The divan or ottoman had been an established furniture form since Regency times, but it took the Aesthetic Movement's fondness for Persian and Indian textiles to nest this cushioned bench, sometimes called a box ottoman, in a bazaar of Oriental stuffs and make it an affectation of bohemian languor, polychromatic decadence, and Moorish comfort. Associated with artist studios, like that of Louis Comfort Tiffany, and art patrons of "advanced" sensibilities, this collection of exotic fabrics, taborets, pierced metal, and old spears was supplied by Liberty of London and other emporiums, and was the ultimate Aesthetic conversation corner.

## CRANE, WALTER

English decorative artist Walter Crane (1845–1915) was a master of design, both two- and three-dimensional. An illustrator of fairy tales and nursery rhymes, he also created textiles, wallpapers, and a host of decorative items in other mediums. He was instrumental in making people more aware of book design, and his work greatly influenced graphic design, especially in American magazines.

**ABOVE:** *In general, the crazy quilt was in its day considered a decorative item rather than a functional one and, if well-made, displayed to advantage the abilities of its maker.* **OPPOSITE PAGE:** *The crinoline, or hoopskirt, looked a lot like a cage.*

## CRAZY QUILTS

The Aesthetic Movement of the 1870s and 1880s, with its encouragement of "art needlework," revived the Colonial American tradition of Moravian silk floss embroidery and applied it to piecing together, with a varied and colorful collection of complex embroidery stitches, a mosaic of elegant and richly colored scraps left over from making drapes, gowns, and upholstery. These mosaics were affectionately called crazy quilts. The manufacturers of silk floss promoted the fashion and stimulated the invention of "crazy quilt stitches." Few of them were intended for use in the bedroom, like the more conservative appliqué and patchwork quilts; most were used as aesthetic accents artfully draped in the late Victorian parlor.

## CRINOLINES

When they appeared in the 1850s, crinolines were hailed as a vast improvement because the stiff fabric made skirts flare without layers of ruffled petticoats. However, there was a slight hitch: they weren't fireproof, and more than one woman was burned to a crisp while cooking dinner or waltzing in a candlelit ballroom. Their replacement, the hoopskirt, or crinoline cage, was made of flexible watch-

spring steel, but it, too, had its problems. Not only were hoopskirts fire traps, they were unwieldy, too. Imagine trying to sit down or waddle through a door without tumbling to the ground while wearing a big, heavy cage around the waist. Finally, crinoline cages were easily soiled and subject to, of all things, rust. But all these problems were not enough to keep women from wearing them or gentlemen from admiring them. In fact, as time went on, hoopskirts became a status symbol and an indication of wealth; the bigger the hoop, the more yards of costly material needed to cover it. Hoopskirts reached their height—and their greatest width—during the Civil War.

## CROCHET

Although it was a single-hook knitting technique practiced before the nineteenth century, crochet reached its peak of development during the Victorian era in Britain and the United States. The best crochet was made in the convent schools of Ireland and was impressively used in bridal gowns, tablecloths, and bedspreads. Its most common use was for doilies, for antimacassars, and for edging the sundry linens required for the proper maintenance of a Victorian household.

## CUCKOO CLOCKS

German Black Forest cuckoo clocks, with their carved walnutlike frames featuring a facade of a simple Swiss chalet infested with vines, leaves, birds, or antlers, ivory hands and numerals, and pinecone weights, were popular Victorian souvenirs as well as a successful export commodity, especially to the United States.

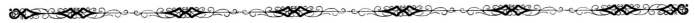

# CURES

While medicine wasn't terribly advanced during the Victorian period, there were many cures on the market, both good and bad. In 1895, for example, there were a variety of cures from which to choose, if the Montgomery Ward & Co. catalog is any indication. Not only did the company sell its own cough syrup ("your physician will tell you that this is one of the best combinations of the pharmacopeia for coughs and colds") for thirty cents a bottle, it also offered sugarcoated Compound Cathartic Pills; Extract Hamamelis (Witch Hazel), a "universal all healing remedy"; Petroleum Pomade (Perfumed), which was like Vaseline; Cook's Eye Water; Cook's Neutralizing Cordial, a laxative; and The Great Russian Corn and Bunion Exterminator that was touted as so effective that "a cure is certain."

## CURRIER & IVES PRINTS

Mother, baseball, apple pie, and Currier & Ives—how much more American can you get? In the nineteenth century, there was nary a parlor that didn't have at least one Currier & Ives lithograph. Why were they so popular? For one thing, they were cheap, and for another, the down-home subjects appealed to the common man. From 1833 to 1906, Nathaniel Currier (1813–1888) and brother-in-law James Ives (1824–1895), New York City printers and publishers, kept American homes supplied with Americana—still lifes, historic and religious scenes, and current events—that are highly collectible today.

## CUT-AND-ENGRAVED GLASS

Cut-and-engraved glass was the gentry's glassware, while pressed-glass pieces comprised the glassware of the more common lot. Many pressed-glass blanks were blown as well as pressed, the telltale lines of the mold cut away during decoration of the surface. At a distance and without strong lighting, it was difficult to tell the difference between cut glass and pressed glass. Most of the intricate patterns of cut glass could be copied by the pressed-glass mold maker. Held in the hand in the proper light the glass was easily identified; the heft of the lead crystal and the brilliance of the faceted surfaces conveyed quality. Some cut-and-engraved glass was intended for display, but much of it was put to use. It is too valuable today for much of it to be used. Like pressed glass, most of it was made as tableware, decorative vessels, and bric-a-brac, but during the 1890s and early twentieth century, it was used to make bases and shades for splendid electric lamps.

## DADO

Originally an exterior architectural feature, the dado moved indoors late in the nineteenth century. "Dado" came to refer to the lower three feet of an interior wall. The dado was topped by the filler and then the frieze. As the nineteenth century progressed, the dado rose until it supplanted the filler.

The dado-filler-frieze pattern for walls was one of the many reforms advocated by Charles Locke Eastlake in his *Hints on Household Taste* (1872). While discussing wallpaper patterns, Eastlake mentions that "paperhangings should in no case be allowed to cover the whole space of the wall from skirting to ceiling. A 'dado' or plinth space of plain colour, should rise to a height of three or four feet from the floor. This may be separated from the diapered paper above by a light wood moulding stained or gilded."

## DAGUERREOTYPE

Named for its inventor, the Frenchman Louis-Jacques-Mandé Daguerre (1789–1851), the daguerreotype introduced photography to the public. Making its appearance only one year after Victoria was crowned, the daguerreotype, with its mirrorlike image, fascinated the Victorians, but it was quite fragile and expensive, and images were easily erased. The snapshot-size daguerreotypes, which were placed under glass and framed in brass, were carried about in cases of leather. People often took their daguerreotypes with them when they traveled so they could gaze at loved ones who were far away. Most daguerreotypes were portraits of individuals, but group portraits and scenic views existed, too.

Matthew Brady, who became famous for the more than 3,500 pictures he took of Civil War sites and heroes (including Abraham Lincoln) in the 1860s, opened a daguerreotype gallery in New York City in 1844 and one in Washington, D.C., in 1847.

By the 1850s, there were two other, more durable alternatives: the ambrotype, introduced by Frederick Scott Archer in England; and the ferrotype, usually called a tintype.

© Robert Perron

**OPPOSITE PAGE:** *Cut-and-engraved glass is still being produced. The most famous company associated with the material is Waterford.* **ABOVE:** *The invention of photography meant that even people of modest means could have their portraits taken. Instead of the wallet snapshot, people carried around daguerreotypes of their loved ones in special leather cases.*

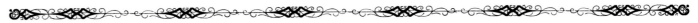

# DECORATIVE ROOFING/SIDING

Textured surfaces were characteristic of late Victorian buildings; these surfaces were sometimes achieved with shingles sawn into diamond butts, octagon butts, half-circle butts (now called "fishscale"), segment butts, and cove butts. The ordinary method was to run a wide band of an ornamental shingle in the middle of a roof completed with square butts or to fill the attic area in a gable with ornamental shingles. Extraordinary results were achieved by combining several varieties in an area. Sometimes these effects were achieved by using slates of various colors. Embossed metal sheets imitating ornamental shingles and slates are still available.

© Robert Perron

# DEPARTMENT STORES

Victorian shopping centers, now called "the old commercial district," have rarely survived in their original splendor. In those areas, the palace of merchant capitalism was the department store. The most successful was A.T. Stewart's in New York City. Famous survivors are John Wanamaker's and Strawbridge & Clothier of Philadelphia, Macy's of New York, and Marshall Field's in Chicago.

# DINING ROOM ART

There was a raging controversy about what was appropriate to feast your eyes on during the dining experience. Some said pictures of dead game were fine; others considered them morbid, saying that paintings that depicted live animals grazing were in much better taste. The same controversy was repeated when it came to carvings of dead fowl on furniture.

# DINING ROOM CONVERSATION

Guests were expected to be brilliant and lively conversationalists, but at the same time had to avoid so many subjects that it is a wonder anyone ever spoke at all during meals. Illnesses, bodily functions, politics, scandals, controversies, accidents, operations, and of course, gossip, were strictly forbidden. (This doesn't even begin to address the difficulties of grappling with all that silverware.)

# DINING ROOM FURNITURE

The center of family life, the dining room had three essential elements, aside from the food: the dining table, which was the honored guest; dining chairs, which were straight-backed and sturdy to aid digestion; and the sideboard, which was part storage compartment, part display cabinet. Dining rooms, in the name of hygiene and germ elimination, were not the most opulent rooms of the house. The upholstery was usually made of leather, and furniture lines were simple.

© Brian Vanden Brink

**OPPOSITE PAGE:** *Elaborately trimmed roofs gave character and prestige to the Victorian house.* **ABOVE:** *The dining room was one of the most important rooms in the house because dinner parties offered excellent opportunities to advance in society. Multi-course meals were standard productions in upper-class and upper-middle-class houses; there was a myriad of rules of etiquette surrounding the dining ritual.*

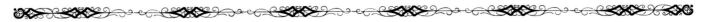

© Balthazar Korab

**ABOVE:** *Even door hinges followed the prevailing decorative styles. This hinge, which is embellished with Japonesque designs, was made late in the century.* **OPPOSITE PAGE:** *The dormers in the Alice Austen House in Staten Island, New York, are decorated with gingerbread. The chimney pots are a quaint touch.*

# DOOR FURNITURE

Aficionados of Victorian hardware catalogs, architectural salvage, and restored entrances find themselves smitten by the visual delights of ironmongery and brasswork. Hinges flash their hidden patterns when opened. Knockers are shaped in the forms of faces, figures, or hands. Bell pulls, house numbers, kick plates, and hand plates are usually highly decorative. Even the doorknobs of the period are remarkably ornate.

# DOOR TEXTS

No Victorian home was complete without a motto or door text, prominently displayed. To welcome guests and to create the right moral atmosphere, the woman of the house was duty-bound to embroider sentimental sayings, frame them, and hang them about, usually over every doorway. The messages were usually sentimental, such as: "Welcome, God Bless Our Home," "Give Us This Day Our Daily Bread," "Thou, God, Seest Me," "The Lord Is My Shepherd," "Peace to This House," and of course "Home, Sweet Home."

# DORMERS

Victorian architects would have agreed with Calvert Vaux's statement in *Villas and Cottages* (1857) that "the sky-line of a building" derives its "picturesqueness by the treatment of the roof-lines." One of the devices used to accomplish this was the dormer window. Vaux said they "are of several sorts, according to the style of the house. They are often made *too* small. A dormer is a capital feature in a country house, and should never be ashamed of itself, or try to shrink out of sight." The word "dormer" is derived from the French word meaning "to sleep"; it is a

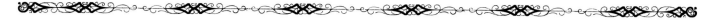

window or door to a dormitory, which the French placed in the attics of buildings. All dormers, therefore, intersect the roof, although some project outward to the plane of the exterior wall and are called wall dormers. They always have sides, or cheeks, and are often ornamented, as Vaux said, in the style of the building they enliven.

## DRESDENS

Miniature cardboard Christmas ornaments made in Germany, Dresdens were embossed in silver and gold and came in a variety of shapes—everything from schools of fish to steamboats. Today, antique Dresdens are considered most desirable as collectibles, and many are being reproduced.

## DRESSER, CHRISTOPHER

A contemporary of William Morris, Christopher Dresser (1834–1904) is known not only for his books on ornamental design but for his wallpapers and fabrics as well. Dresser was trained as a botanist, and his naturalistic patterns are extremely detailed. An industrial designer, Dresser worked with Josiah Wedgwood & Sons Ltd. and with Minton and Co., which made decorative tiles.

## DRUGGET

A cloth placed under the dining table to protect the carpet and to catch crumbs, the drugget took on a slightly different function as the century progressed. Late in the era, instead of covering a rug, it became the only floor covering, and was placed atop wooden or parquet flooring. Woven flannel or painted burlap were two recommended drugget fabrics.

## DUST CORNERS

In their never-ending quest to make cleaning easier, the Victorians of the 1890s introduced dust corners, triangular pieces of wood that were attached to the corners of staircases to catch—what else?—dust. The corners soon became more decorative, and embossed brass was substituted for wood. It is questionable whether they made the stairs easier to clean, but they did make them more attractive. Dust corners are still being made.

Because of *Household Taste*, which covered the design of everything from door knockers and lace curtains to jewelry, boots, and hats, Eastlake's name became a household word, and everybody wanted Eastlake furniture. Furniture makers were only too happy to oblige, and soon factories were churning out all sorts of so-called "Eastlake furniture" that in general violated every rule in *Household Taste*. Even though Eastlake issued a public disclaimer, the public continued to buy the merchandise.

## EASTLAKE FURNITURE

Technically speaking, there is no such thing as Eastlake furniture. For although the English architect Charles Locke Eastlake (1836–1906) had very definite ideas about furniture reform and even wrote them down in his *Hints on Household Taste* (1872), he never made any furniture and nobody else executed his ideas correctly. And Eastlake's ideas, for the most part, were not even new. Others had been proposing the same reforms, but Eastlake was the first to set them down in a manner that caught the attention of the general public.

Eastlake's book was a great success, and everybody wanted the furniture he described. Referring back to the Middle Ages, when handcrafting was an art, he advocated furniture that was "plain and straightforward" and "strong and comely," not flimsily "elegant and light." To this end, he disdained veneers, varnish, scrolling C- and S-curves, machine-made and applied ornament and graining, and all furniture of a "medley of styles." His "pure style" modern furniture, constructed in accordance with medieval design, was to be angular in shape and decorated with incised carving, marquetry, or wooden inlays. And unlike the other Art Furniture of the day, it was to be inexpensive. "Every article of furniture should," he wrote, "at the first glance, proclaim its real purpose."

## EBONIZED FURNITURE

Although John Henry Belter displayed an ebonized table at the New York Crystal Palace Exhibition in 1853, ebonized furniture did not come into its own until the Aesthetic Movement of the 1870s and 1880s was in full swing. The process of ebonizing, or staining wood black to simulate ebony, was applied to entire pieces of furniture or only to parts to emphasize certain decorative elements, like finials. It was used with dramatic effect in combination with incising and gilding.

**OPPOSITE PAGE:** *Charles Locke Eastlake never made any furniture, but many manufacturers misinterpreted his popular ideas and churned out pieces that they presumptuously called Eastlake. Most pieces of Victorian furniture are an amalgam of styles, as is this bed, which most probably could be classified as Renaissance Revival. Undoubtedly, it would have been advertised as Eastlake in the nineteenth century.*
**ABOVE:** *Victorian ebonized furniture, such as this Kimble & Cabus cabinet, is highly desirable. This spectacular piece is in the collection of antiques dealer Stingray Hornsby of Watertown, Connecticut.*

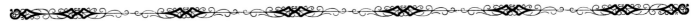

# EDGING PLANTS

"Almost every day some one inquires what is best for a low edging for flower beds," said *Vick's Flower and Vegetable Garden* (1878). "For a summer edging almost any low growing, compact plant will answer—anything either pretty in foliage or in flowers. What is generally desired is a permanent border." Vick's recommended *Amerio vulgaris*, or thrift. "For a low, white edging or border, the Alyssum is excellent." Annual varieties of lobelia are "freely used as edgings for beds of ornamental-leaved and other bedding plants."

# EGYPTIAN REVIVAL

The Victorians were fascinated by the exotic, so it is hardly surprising that the motifs of ancient Egypt, including sphinxes and pyramids, caught their eye and were translated into a style of decoration. In the nineteenth century, ancient Egypt was considered the oldest civilization, the forerunner of all others.

Although Napoleon had waged Egyptian campaigns in the 1790s, and several temples had been uncovered early in the period, it was not until the Suez Canal opened in 1869 and the Centennial Exhibition opened in 1876 that the Egyptian Revival really began in earnest. A visit to Egypt's exhibit at that event—a rendition of an ancient temple that was supported by columns whose capitals were the lotus flower—was likened to a visit to the land of the *Arabian Nights*. Soon afterward, motifs of the Nile—the sphinx, obelisk, scarab, papyrus plant, the lotus flower, and even hieroglyphics—started showing up on everything from furniture mounts and wallpapers to mantel garnitures, tea sets, jewelry, and flatware. The revival got another boost in 1893 when Egypt set up another temple decorated with a sphinx and pyramids at the World's Columbian Exposition in Chicago.

Although a few wealthy individuals decorated their mansions in the Egyptian style, it was never that popular, and surviving furniture and decorative accessories are considered rare and extremely valuable.

When Americans weren't carting back ancient treasures from Egypt—the obelisk, including the one in New York City's Central Park, was the most famous monument ever taken—they were erecting Nile-inspired monuments in, of all places, cemeteries.

# ELECTRICAL JEWELS

Once Edison switched on the light bulb, he opened up a whole new world of ideas. Everybody, it seemed, wanted to get in on the act. Monsieur G. Trouve of Paris came up with what he thought was a brilliant idea: jewels that light up. His artificial jewels, he claimed, were far superior to diamonds because their light came from within, thereby being constant.

Intended to be worn mainly by stars of the stage, they could be used as buttons, hairpins, tiepins, scarfpins, or even knobs of walking sticks. And they supposedly did wonders for bouquets. They weren't as magical as they seemed; each electrical jewel, which shone for up to a half hour, contained a tiny light bulb that was connected to a lightweight battery. Lest you think this was all in jest, it was recorded that none other than Mrs. Cornelius Vanderbilt was spotted tripping the light fantastic in a blue "electric light" ballgown in 1883 (it was designed by the famous French couturier Charles Frederick Worth).

# ELECTRIC LIGHTING

Gas lighting was such an improvement that no one fore-saw that electricity would supplant it, and certainly not as early as the 1880s and 1890s. Because electricity was an uncertain quantity, the first electric fixtures, which looked like gasoliers, were combined with gas, which was used as a backup energy source. Victorians loved to show off any type of new technology, and the first totally electric fix-tures, bare bulbs placed in porcelain sockets or suspended from the ceiling by wires, were considered quite chic.

**OPPOSITE PAGE:** *Egyptian Revival pieces, such as this Pottier & Stymus armchair, are rare. This piece belongs to antiques dealer Stingray Hornsby of Watertown, Connecticut.* **ABOVE:** *When it was introduced, electric lighting caused quite a sensation for many reasons. It not only changed the way people lived, but it changed the way rooms — and people — looked. Everything from makeup to architectural color schemes had to be adjusted.*

# ELIZABETHAN REVIVAL FURNITURE

A.J. Downing and other early Victorian promoters of the Gothic Revival in the United States treated the Elizabethan Revival as a handmaiden of Gothic Revival, but it turned out to be more generally popular than its master. Its distinguishing mark was the use of the spiral turning, which was much easier and cheaper to make than the carved pinnacles and molded, recessed, pointed-arch panels characteristic of Gothic Revival furniture. Spirals were readily converted to spools by mechanized carving machines, and in this form the Elizabethan Revival survived throughout the nineteenth century. After it became known that Jenny Lind, "The Swedish Nightingale" ballyhooed by P.T. Barnum in her triumphal American tour, slept in a spool bed, the Jenny Lind Bed became a staple of Victorian furniture showrooms. The simplest explanation for the success of Elizabethan and the failure of Gothic Revival is that women of the Victorian era preferred the former and disliked the latter.

© Balthazar Korab

# ENCAUSTIC TILES

The making of encaustic tiles, a long-forgotten medieval art, was revived in the 1830s in England by Minton and Co. After a dozen years of experimentation, Minton began selling these colorful, unglazed floor tiles, which remained popular until the turn of the century. In 1843, after Prince Albert ordered them for Osborne House, on the Isle of Wight, everybody else in the empire had to have them, too.

# ENGAGEMENT RINGS

A diamond, which symbolized innocence, was what every bride wanted to wear on her finger, but there were other choices that could be used alone or in combination with that coveted stone. And in that most sentimental of eras, each stone was assigned a meaning. Sapphires meant immortal life, rubies represented affection, and emeralds brought success in love. Pearls and opals were avoided as they were considered harbingers of ill luck. Sometimes couples chose a variety of stones, using the first letter of each to spell out the name of the bride or even to create their own private messages. All of this was—and still is—considered terribly romantic.

# ENTRANCES/DOORS/PORCHES

Calvert Vaux, in *Villas and Cottages* (1857), listed "the principal features of detail that occur in country residences" and said that "the *porch*, or *entrance*, suggests itself as having the priority of claim." Note that a porch is a projection in front of a door or entrance and is scaled in relationship to it. "A large house," said Vaux, "may be spoiled by a mean porch, and the interior effect of a small, compact house will appear dwarfed and contracted if it is approached through a pretentious entrance-porch." Like

dormers, porches were usually ornamentalized in the style of the house, sometimes including a canopy or hood projecting over the door instead of a porch enclosure. Entrances were also decorated with brass letter slots, postboxes, numerals, bell-pulls, door knockers, and ornamental hardware. Transoms and sidelights, as well as the glass in the door, could be plain, beveled plate, leaded, stained, transfer-printed, etched, engraved, or flashed and cut-to-clear. An ornamental, but functional, boot-scraper was essential to cope with the ubiquitous mud of Victorian roads and streets.

© D.E. Cox

**OPPOSITE PAGE:** *Encaustic tiles proved particularly serviceable and beautiful for entrance halls and vestibules.* **ABOVE:** *The Victorians liked to make grand entrances.*

## EPERGNE

A dining table centerpiece, an epergne was a glass or silver bowl that had a series of baskets or V-shaped vessels that could hold anything from fresh flowers to fresh fruits, nuts, sweets, or even holly at Christmastime. By the 1870s, even wax food found a place in the epergne. Another one of the many Victorian status symbols, the epergne was to be lavishly decorated so as to impress dinner guests.

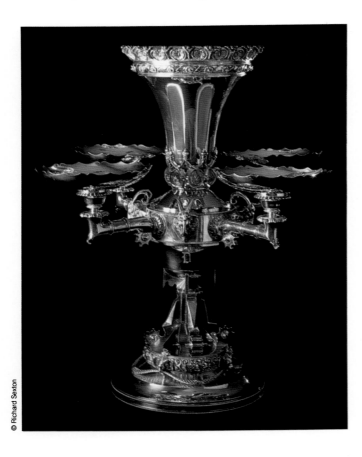

© Richard Sexton

## ETAGERE

The fancy cousin of the whatnot, an étagère is a display piece of furniture with a large central mirror flanked by a series of small, graduated shelves and a couple of full-size shelves below the mirror. Its shelves were usually filled with all manner of objects, turning it into a miniature museum.

## EVERGREENS

Frank J. Scott, in his *Art of Beautifying Surburban Home Grounds* (1870), makes the sage observation that evergreens are least attractive after their first twenty years of growth. He implies that they should be replaced at maturity, "when most of them become more rigid and monotonous in outline, and less cheerful in expression than the average deciduous trees." The first landscape chore facing new owners of neglected Victorian properties is removing overgrown evergreens. Perhaps one or two of the healthiest and most attractively positioned evergreens might be kept as specimen trees; the others should be replaced, for the original effect of their planting is long gone.

## EVERLASTING FLOWERS

According to Edward Sprague Rand's *Flowers for the Parlor and Garden* (1864), "These flowers lessen the regret we all feel when the season of blooms is over, because they enable us to transfer a little of summer beauty to the parlor. They retain both form and color for years, and make excellent [dried-flower] bouquets, wreaths and many other desirable winter ornaments. Those who are familiar with the usual style of winter holiday decoration, and realize how gloomy a room is made by the heavy, dark wreaths of cedars and hemlocks, unrelieved by a flower or berry, or any bright color, will thank us for urging them to save every flower that will keep its color during the winter. Make all wreaths light and airy, and enliven them with bright colors."

**ABOVE:** *The epergne was usually filled with fruit or flowers and was used as a centerpiece on the dining table.* **OPPOSITE PAGE:** *Everlasting flowers or dried flowers were often turned into wreaths and other winter ornaments. Here, in a modern setting, dried flowers are used as a decorative motif over a mantel. The Victorians would not have used them this way.*

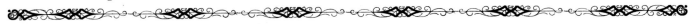

# EXHIBITION BUILDINGS

Well into the twentieth century, most county fairgrounds and their exhibition buildings survived, along with a dirt track for horse-racing. The most famous Victorian exhibition buildings are those of the International Expositions, beginning in 1851 with Sir Joseph Paxton's Crystal Palace in London, which survived until 1936, when it burned down. New York's Crystal Palace of 1853, with its splendid colored glass and gaslighting, was influential for a time, but it burned down in 1858. Dublin's exhibition of 1853 was largely a local affair. In 1855, the Paris exhibition was famous for the visit of Victoria and Albert, the first by a reigning English monarch in three hundred years. The London exhibition of 1862 was saddened by the death of Albert. The Paris exhibition of 1867 is remembered for the engineering feats of Alexandre Gustave Eiffel; this was followed by exhibitions in London (1871–1874) and Vienna (1873). The United States put on a world-class Centennial Exposition in 1876 in Philadelphia's Fairmount Park. (The only surviving exhibition building from that event is the Art Gallery, now called Memorial Hall.) The 1878 Paris exhibition established a new attendance record; the 1889

Paris exhibition is best known for Eiffel's tower. In 1893, the Chicago exhibition opened during a devastating worldwide economic depression; it was famous for its Beaux Arts Dream City, superintended by Daniel H. Burnham, which used designs by Richard Morris Hunt, Stanford White, and Louis Sullivan. The Paris exhibition of 1900 brought the century to a close and was the last great international exposition of arts and manufacture.

# EXTENSION TABLES

Progressive designers of the late Victorian decades despised the extension table because they considered the table dishonest. Few Victorians, however, could afford a large enough dining room to permit the permanent residence of a full-length table. Nor could they afford a separate room for more intimate family dining. The extension dining table satisfied an essential requirement of middle-class Victorian living and entertaining, so a great deal of inventiveness was often displayed in its mechanisms. Similar tables are still being made today.

© Archive Photos

# EXTERIOR COLORS

The key concept of selecting and placing Victorian exterior paint colors was imitation. Paint was applied to cheap materials to make them look like more expensive materials, hence the popularity of paint colors that imitated building stones, hardwoods, metals, tiles, terra-cotta, and bricks. This practice was well established prior to the 1840s, when Andrew Jackson Downing ridiculed the white walls and green blinds of American neoclassical buildings. White walls, which were a yellowish-white from the linseed oil resin in common use, imitated

© Robert Perron

Ancient Greek and Roman marbles; green blinds imitated Renaissance bronze shutters. Calvert Vaux's *Villas and Cottages* (1857) recommended a four-color scheme. "The walls should be of some agreeable shade of color; the roof-trimmings, verandas, and other woodwork being either of a different color or of a different shade of the same color, so that a contrast, but not a harsh one, may be established. The third color, not widely different from the other wood-work, should be applied to the solid parts of the Venetian blinds, and the movable slats should be painted of the fourth tint…by far the darkest used on the premises, for the effect of a glass window or opening in a wall is always dark when seen from a distance." Vaux said the last color was important "when the blinds are closed, which is most of the time." The best general advice appeared in Frank J. Scott's *Art of Beautifying Suburban Home Grounds* (1870): "Colors which appear to have no character at all on small surfaces, are often beautiful when applied to an entire building; while tints which please us best in samples may be rank and vulgar on broad surfaces." After the Civil War, America's infant ready-mixed paint companies positioned their new product in the marketplace by promoting inno-vative colors in new combinations for the increasingly ornamented exteriors of late Victorian architecture. "Pick-ing out," or accenting the bumps and grinds of architec-tural detailing was advocated in the beautifully illustrated product literature of ready-mixed paint companies. Since 1975, Devoe has made available its Traditions line of col-ors, which reproduces colors promoted in a gorgeous countertop display book of 1885 titled *Exterior Decoration*. In 1981, Sherwin-Williams made available its Heritage Colors, 1820–1920, which has been revised and expanded in 1991 as its Preservation Palette, 1820–1970.

**OPPOSITE PAGE:** *The International Exposition of 1853 was housed in this magnificent structure, which was (like the exposition itself) a tribute to the achievements of an industrializing world.* **ABOVE:** *The exteriors of Victorian homes were graced with many charming architectural details; the availability of a variety of ready-mixed paints made it possible for nineteenth-century home owners to bring out these details with lively color schemes.*

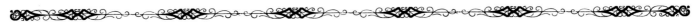

# FACTORIES/MILLS/WAREHOUSES

"No single building type," states Robert M. Vogel in *Built in the U.S.A.* (1985), "exists in a greater profusion of scales, shapes, materials, and other variables than industrial structures." Some of the most successful architectural preservation efforts have resulted in the adaptive reuse of industrial structures, often as apartments, retail shops, studios, or museums. The Chickering Piano Factory (1853) in Boston was converted into apartment/studios for artists. The Lone Star Brewing Company (1895) is now the San Antonio Museum of Art. A candy factory complex in San Francisco has been converted into the popular attraction called Ghirardelli Square. The most famous early Victorian industrial complex was the mill town of Lowell, Massachusetts. The best-known warehouse is Henry Hobson Richardson's Marshall Field and Company Wholesale House (1887) in Chicago.

# FAIRY LAMPS

It seems incredible that during the second half of the nineteenth century when gaslighting and kerosene lighting had made candlepower obsolete, and even during the 1880s when electric lighting began to be used, that any candle-burning device could compete. When Samuel

Clarke patented a slow-burning candle in 1857, sold it in a fancy holder as a night light for nurseries or bedrooms, and named it a "fairy lamp," he was able to compete. The candle remained an obsolete device, but Clarke and his imitators capitalized on the reverse snobbery of using it as well as the romanticism of its illumination, which was enhanced by fancy ceramic or glass shades and holders purchased from some of the leading manufacturers of the day. They were also used in parlors, dining rooms, and conservatories, and outside in the garden. They continued to be made well into the twentieth century and were subsequently collected as examples of fancy Victorian glass and china. Today they are too valuable to use, and so it is left to reproduction luminaria to provide romantic lighting for late Victorian interiors.

**ABOVE:** *The Industrial Revolution brought with it factories, mills, and warehouses, but the Victorian love of decoration didn't spill over into the industrial sector. Even in Victorian times, industrial buildings were considered strictly utilitarian. Many were sweatshops.* **OPPOSITE PAGE:** *Fences sported some of the most delightful and fanciful designs of the period and often coordinated with the rest of the architectural decoration.*

## FANS

Hand-held fans were far more than a decorative accessory or a device for reviving the more-than-occasional swooning ballroom dancer. Long before Sally Rand, they were a not-so-secret way to flirt legitimately. Although it is questionable how much of this flirting was actually carried out, there were all sorts of complex rules about the meaning of the position of the fan when held in the hand of the young woman. If the woman fanned fast, she was conveying her independence; if she fanned slowly, she signaled that she was already engaged. A fan with the right hand in front of her face encouraged advances, while when done with the left it recommended retreat. An open fan meant love, a closed one hate. While a half-open fan signaled friendship, a swinging one sang out, "Walk me home." And the best, of course, was the fan that opened and shut, for it meant, "Oh kiss me, please, please, please."

Women also had a large selection of fans from which to choose. Bloomingdale's Illustrated 1886 Catalog shows eleven of them, some made with satin and trimmed with feathers. The Telescope Fan, which sold for fifteen to forty-nine cents, depending on whether it was ordered in alligator, velvet, satin, plush, or Russian leather, was not only "entirely new," it was "handy for pocket use" because of the compact manner in which it folded up.

## FEATHER TREES

Introduced in Germany late in the eighteenth century, the first artificial Christmas trees became popular during the last part of the Victorian era. Branches made of turkey or goose feathers dyed green or even white were stuck into a trunk. By today's standards, this method makes a very sparse-looking tree indeed.

© Robert Perron

## FENCES

The function of most Victorian fences in the vicinity of Victorian homes had more to do with exterior horticultural decoration than exterior architectural decoration. Frank J. Scott's *Art of Beautifying Suburban Home Grounds* (1870) said "that kind of fence is best which is least seen, and best seen through." Scott said to avoid repeating veranda railings as fences, especially "boards sawed so that their openings form ornamental designs. These are adopted from German designs for cheap balconies and veranda guards, but for front fences they are even more objectionable than pickets, because they bar more completely the view of what is behind." Scott's ideal fence was made of ornamental cast-iron posts linked by six or seven widely spaced horizontal iron rods.

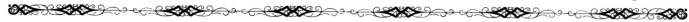

## FERNERIES

The most popular use of the Wardian Case or terrarium was for growing ferns, which guidebooks like Henry T. Williams' *Window Gardening for Parlor Decoration* (1871) called fern cases. The fernery, or fern case, looked like a simple aquarium with a glass lid, and could be made at home. For the ambitious fern grower, Williams illustrated a fern window—a window space given over completely to an aquarium at the bottom, out of which rose a miniature rockery supporting a collection of ferns. Ferns were also grown outside glass cases. Williams illustrates "*Rustic Terra Cotta Arborettes* cast in rugged form resembling the projecting limbs of an oak tree just clipped, and with cavities opening downward for the reception of earth and holding plants."

## FILLER

In the 1870s, there was yet another reform movement afoot. Tastemakers were reevaluating the prevailing style and were finding it wanting in many respects. Charles Locke Eastlake, in his *Hints on Household Taste* (1872), advocated dividing the walls of the house into three parts and putting separate wallpapers on each, because "the most dreary method of decorating a wall of the sitting-room is to cover it all with an unrelieved pattern of monotonous design." Starting from the floor and working his way up, he specified a dado, a filler, and a frieze.

Filler papers were generally adorned with small, overall repeating patterns because they were intended to innocuously fill the space between the more flamboyant dado and frieze. Furthermore, since the filler was where pictures were hung, such a background wouldn't clash with the artwork.

© Robert Perron

## FINGER BOWLS

When it came to dining, there were all manner of rules and all manner of utensils to master. In general, fingers and food were not to touch in polite company, but if a diner should be careless, dirty digits could be dipped in a finger bowl. A tip of a linen napkin dipped into the water in the finger bowl could be used to wipe the lips. A finger bowl doily placed under the bowl not only protected the finish of the table but provided a cloth for wiping fingers. One had to hope that such aid was not necessary early in the meal, however, for the finger bowl usually didn't make its appearance until the fruit and dessert course.

**OPPOSITE PAGE:** *The filler wallpaper in this sewing room is decorated with rustic frames and a Japonesque fan. It coordinates with but does not match the dado paper below.* **ABOVE:** *Ferns — both indoors and outdoors — were key elements in Victorian decorative designs. Hanging ferns are still as popular as they were during the last century. Ferns were often placed in beautiful majolica jardinieres, then set atop pedestals in the parlor*

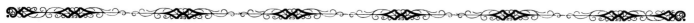

## FIREHOUSES

For much of the nineteenth century, institutionalized fire-fighting organizations were more effective as social and political clubs than they were at fighting fires. As cities grew, especially after the Civil War, fire fighting became a paid profession, but the volunteer fire company remained (and still remains) a potent political force in rural and smaller communities. The storage of pumpers and steam engines, the stabling of horses, the maintenance of club-rooms or dormitories for firemen, and, after 1840, the construction of drying towers for hoses required special internal arrangements. Externally, firehouses were built in the popular architectural styles of their day and were identifiable by the wide openings on the ground floor.

© Gross & Daley

## FIREPLACE EQUIPMENT

Because the symbolic importance of "the ancestral hearth" became more important after the Victorian perfection of central heating, fireplace equipment became more elaborate and stylish as the open fireplace became obsolete. Coal scuttles, grates, fenders, firebacks, firedogs, kettles, and tool sets were representative of the fashions of the day.

## FLOORCLOTHS

From the 1830s through the 1850s, high-traffic areas of the house were sometimes covered with floorcloths, canvas cloths sized with several coats of oil paint on each side, then painted with patterns that mocked real carpets or floor tiles. They were expensive but lasted for years, and many homeowners had home recipes for making them. By the mid-nineteenth century, they were called oilcloths.

© D.E. Cox

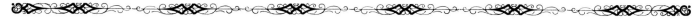

# FLORAL DECORATION

"Flowers, like people, have places where they do themselves and their friends credit, while in other situations there is general disappointment and mortification," according to *Vick's Flower and Vegetable Garden* (1878). The floral decoration of a Victorian interior was not expected to survive the event it helped celebrate. Present-day expectations for floral decorations lasting days or weeks are far more romantic in comparison with the Victorian acceptance of reality. Once the initial impression had been made and one's guests comprehended that all of the fragile and momentary floral decorations had been made just for them, Victorian entertainers were not in the least upset by subsequent fading and wilting during the event. This attitude also explains the Victorian use of seasonal floral decoration. If it came from one's own estate or garden, so much the better. The most common form of interior decoration with plant material for special occasions was the swagging, festooning, or wreathing of cornices, ceilings, windows, drapes, doors, exposed picture wires, and lighting fixtures with laurel, ivy, or smilax.

© Nancy Hill

**OPPOSITE PAGE, LEFT:** *Every able-bodied man was expected to help fight fires, and firehouses often took on the air of social clubs.* **OPPOSITE PAGE, RIGHT:** *Fireplace screens such as this one were often more decorative than useful.* **ABOVE:** *The Victorians cherished flowers and filled their rooms with live blooms and representations of them. Chintz fabrics and pillows were bright counterpoints to dreary winters.*

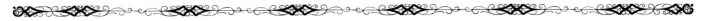

# FLOWER BOXES

These were popular Victorian interior and exterior devices for floral decoration. "Those who are not fortunate enough to have balconies, can find very handsome window boxes of beautiful patterns," said *Vick's Flower and Vegetable Garden* (1878). "But one may easily and cheaply make a good, durable window box. A common box, the length of the window, about eight inches deep and ten inches wide, can be fastened on the outside of the window by means of either iron or wood brackets. This may be painted, or, what is still better, covered with oil cloth. Get some small, set figure, and you have an imitation of a tile box at very little cost." For window boxes Vick's recommended geraniums, lobelias, *Vinca variegata*, sweet alyssum, othomna, ivy geraniums, *Convolvulus mauritanicus*, thunbergias, tropaeolum, maurandya, *Calanpelis scabra*, and German ivies. A popular use for an interior window box was as a miniature bulb garden.

**ABOVE:** *Flower boxes were used to liven up exteriors and interiors. Live flowers were treasured for their fleeting beauty.* **RIGHT:** *Footstools came in a variety of styles and prices.* **OPPOSITE PAGE:** *Fountains were prominent not only in public places, but in homes as well. It was not uncommon to see a fountain in a conservatory.*

# FOOD

To the Victorians, a full larder was a sign of prosperity, so it is no surprise that they used the technology of the Industrial Revolution to fill their pantries. It was during this era that canned goods and other processed foods—condensed milk, ketchup, sardines, preserves, pickles, soups—made their appearance and radically altered what the middle class put in their stomachs. The advent of the factory, along with improvements in growing methods and in transportation (primarily the refrigerated rail car), made many more fresh, out-of-season foods available to the general public. Bananas, oranges, celery, refined white sugar, cream, and butter became readily available, and created the market for all kinds of fancy glass and silver dishes to display them. Today's nutritionists scorn Victorian diets, calling them unhealthy. And one needs only read Upton Sinclair's *The Jungle* to get an idea of what the meat-packing industry was really putting on turn-of-the-century tables.

# FOOTSTOOLS

Victorians knew how to put their feet up in style. They used footstools, which were made at all times in every style from cheap homemade to expensive architect-designed. They were fair game for the needleworking skills of the household and were often given tops of Berlin wool work. So many were made that they are the cheapest and most readily available article of Victorian furniture today.

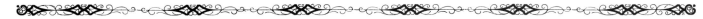

## FOUNTAINS

Italian fountains of the Renaissance and Baroque eras were objects of fascination for Victorians. Fountains were installed as elegant symbols of gentility in civic centers, public parks, residential districts within a city, suburban villas, and country houses. Although the biggest ones are magnificent combinations of architecture and sculpture, no fountain can come to life without water under pressure and an audience to appreciate its magic. Victorian manufacturers of cast-iron items produced small and medium-sized fountains, the most sentimental of which was a little boy and girl beneath an umbrella with a jet of water at its tip. Some owners of Victorian homes avoid Victorian fountains because the metal sculptures and basins are expensive, but the pleasures of having a fountain can be achieved less dearly with a simple geometric basin placed on or sunk in the ground, a single jet slightly above the water level, and a recirculating pump. When such a feature is placed in a quiet area of the landscape and is partially surrounded by plantings that contain and amplify the soothing sound of splashing water, it is a delight for family and friends.

## FRETWORK

Fretwork went by various names, including Sorrento carving and jigsaw work. After it was showcased at the 1876 Philadelphia Centennial by Henry T. Williams, who published three hundred patterns for it in *Ornamental Designs for Fret-Work, Fancy Carving and Home Decorations* (1875), it became a popular domestic art for both men and women. Thin sheets of wood were used to make silhouettelike designs. Some of the items for which Williams provided designs were small easels, work baskets, watch pockets, matchboxes, inkstands, letter openers, penholder bearers, towel racks, calendar frames, lamp screens, crosses, photograph frames, book racks, and

© Nance S. Trueworthy

*Fretwork*

🔲 **ABOVE:** *Fretwork panels decorate the stairway of this Victorian home.* **OPPOSITE PAGE, TOP AND BOTTOM:** *This Renaissance Revival jewel box/candelabra and this Pottier & Stymus neoclassical hall table (complete with hoofed feet) would have made strange but not uncommon partners in the Victorian age, when a single room sometimes featured the full spectrum of nineteenth-century styles.*

© Nancy Hill; Design: Nauticone and Associates

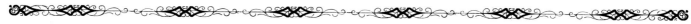

small brackets. Large jigsaws and bandsaws were used to make similar but larger exterior scrollwork brackets, peak ornaments, and cresting ornaments for verandas and gables (late Victorians called such ornamentation "cornice drapery" and it is now known as gingerbread). Most fretwork was deliberately destroyed, or disintegrated with use, but reproductions can be made cheaply with today's laser-cutting machines.

## FRIEZE

In the three-part wall division introduced in the 1870s, the frieze was the wide border closest to the ceiling. In his *Hints on Household Taste* (1872), Charles Locke Eastlake writes, "A second space, of frieze, left just below the ceiling, and filled with arabesque ornament painted on a distemper ground, is always effective, but of course involves some additional expense."

The divisions of the tripartite wall could be delineated with wooden railings or with special wallpapers that imitated the three divisions. Several designers, including Christopher Dresser and Walter Crane, made these papers.

## FURNITURE

The word "eclectic" has often been applied to the Victorian period in general, and to its furnishings in particular, with good reason. During a reign that technically spanned more than six decades but whose influence lasted far longer, the world changed drastically—and so did styles. The Victorians have been accused of being borrowers of styles, and while that is true, it should also be noted that they never copied styles exactly but simply used elements of them to develop their own unique revivals—Rococo, Renaissance, Gothic, and Egyptian, to name a few. Sometimes the results were stunning; other times they were disasters.

The Victorians also tended to hold on to what they had. As styles changed, they may have added a couple of pieces to their homes, but these new additions were placed right next to the furniture they bought when they got married. This, of course, made homes look very eclectic, indeed.

Up until the 1970s, Victorian furniture was considered too fussy to fit into a modern lifestyle. In the last two decades, however, the value of such furniture has not only been recognized but legitimized by the prices the pieces bring. (Furniture in earlier Victorian styles, particularly Rococo Revival pieces, first attracted all the attention, but later pieces have recently come into their own.) As is true of any period, the best pieces bring the best prices. In general, brand-name pieces—Belter, Meeks, Herter Brothers, Pottier & Stymus, and so on—that were expensive when they were made are costly today, too. (For example, in 1990, a splendid Herter Brothers parlor table sold for $280,000, a record for a Victorian piece, and a highly carved rosewood Belter bed topped the $100,000 mark, a record for a Belter piece.)

It should also be noted that certain styles are popular in certain parts of the country. For instance, in the South, where the Civil War froze styles, Rococo Revival pieces are the most popular and most pricey, while on the East Coast, collectors pay a premium for Aesthetic Movement pieces.

than 45 degrees. The raking eaves of Victorianized medieval styles often are ornamented with cornice drapery called "peak ornaments" and verge-boards or barge-boards. The raking eaves of neoclassical styles are ornamented by bracketed entablatures, paneled friezes, and pendant cornice trimmings that look like lace. In both categories the eaves sometimes end in a shallow curve to give what is now called a bell-cast profile.

## GABLES

Gables are usually triangular in outline, unless they are "clipped" with a hipped roof at the top, have raking curvilinear baroque parapets, end in a gambrel or double-pitched roof, or terminate in a shallow curved roof. The gables of Gothic Revival and other Victorianized medieval styles tend to have roofs pitched more than 45 degrees. The gables of neoclassical styles tend to be pitched less

## GARDEN SEATING AND TABLES

Victorians conceived of their gardens as outdoor living spaces, hence the tendency to make them look like outdoor parlors decorated with the colorful ruffles and flourishes of flowers and shrubs, and furnished accordingly with chairs, circular seats, bench-sofas, and tables made of wood, wrought iron, cast-iron, or wire. Such associations were enhanced by the reproduction of indoor parlor chairs in cast-iron for use in these outdoor parlors.

## GARDEN TOOLS AND ACCESSORIES

With the Victorian revival in houses and gardens has come a revival of interest in Victorian hand tools and garden accessories. A mail-order company of the present day, Smith and Hawken, began its march to success by reviving traditional gardener's shovels, spades, and forks in common use by Victorian gardeners. Scythes, which were used to cut large areas of Victorian estate grounds as well as fields of grain, have been revived as part of an ecologically prudent technology. Hand-powered reel mowers, invented in the nineteenth century, have been revived for the same reason.

© Balthazar Korab

© Nancy Hill; Courtesy of House Beautiful's Home Remodeling and Decorating

## GASLIGHTING

Because kerosene lighting was for the people, Victorian gentry associated themselves with gaslighting, which required in-house gas-making machinery before the development of municipal gasworks and pipelines. The best document of a fashionable house converting from kerosene to gas is the frontispiece to *American Woman's Home* (1869), by Beecher and Stowe. The harp of an obsolete kerosene hanging light has been retained in the parlor to support a rustic adornment of a bird's nest with stuffed birds in it. A gas table lamp illuminates the family reading circle, and the gas is delivered obtrusively via a rubber hose connected to a nipple in the wall. Gaslighting survives, of course, as romantic street lighting in historic districts and trendy shopping areas. This does not, however, reveal the full effects of interior gaslighting in Victorian homes. Our perceptions of most fashionable Victorian interiors at night would be dramatically altered if we could view them illuminated by their original gaslights. We wouldn't soon forget the singular aroma, either.

## GARDEN UTILITY BUILDINGS

"The stable, the wood-shed, the well-house, the tool-room, and all needful back buildings," wrote Frank J. Scott in *Art of Beautifying Suburban Home Grounds* (1870), "should be made with as much reference to good taste in their design as the dwelling, and should all have the same general architectural character." Potting sheds were sometimes located in the back of the backhouse, or outdoor toilet. Victorian families who couldn't afford the benefits of commercial refrigeration and regular delivery of manufactured ice had ice houses for the storage of natural winter ice cut from ponds, lakes, and rivers. Victorian doghouses were sometimes built as tiny cottages. Tents for temporary purposes were placed on the lawn, especially for garden parties, socials, and weddings. Scott suggested "A gray or cool drab-colored house should not have a warm brown color for its outbuildings. A cream-colored house should have its outbuildings of some darker shade, in which yellow is just perceptible as one of its constituent parts. In places where they are much shaded by trees, the outbuildings may be the color of the dwelling, provided the latter is some un-showy neutral tint."

**OPPOSITE PAGE:** *Gables were often highly decorated with gingerbread fretwork.* **ABOVE, LEFT:** *The Victorians developed a whole set of furniture styles that they felt were particularly appropriate to the garden. Rustic wire and wicker were the mainstays then, and today many of the same styles are still in vogue.* **ABOVE:** *Gaslights were a vast improvement over candles and kerosene lamps, but in the beginning they were not dependable. Reproductions of many Victorian-style gas fixtures such as this one are much sought after by people restoring nineteenth-century houses.*

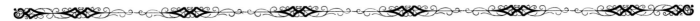

# GATES

"A gateway, whether for a carriage road or a well," wrote Frank J. Scott in his *Art of Beautifying Suburban Home Grounds* (1870), "should always be marked in some way, so that one will know at a glance, and at some distance, just where the entrance is." Scott went on to castigate those gates that were "pretentious," had a "cheap showiness," or had a "massiveness disproportionate to their importance." Of the gateposts, which were made of stone, brick, cast-iron, or wood, Scott said they did not have to be the same size, because only one had to bear the weight of the gate and children who swing on it. Scott preferred arched natural gateways (without gates) that led through specially planted and carefully trained shrubs or trees to architectural gateways with gates. A cheap but effective Victorian device for verdant gateways was a wire arch about a foot in depth, which provided a trellis for plants. When several of these were distributed throughout the landscape, they became verdant arbors or bowers. Arranged in a circle, they became verdant gazebos or summerhouses.

# GAZEBOS/SUMMERHOUSES

Gazebos are fashionable additions to present-day landscapes, whether there is a Victorian building nearby or not. In most instances, they are expensive objects of architectural sculpture with a low occupancy rate and little to look at when inhabited. Victorians called them summerhouses, a term that indicates their frequent use during the warm months of the year. "The Summer-house may cost but little; indeed more depends upon the situation, tastefulness of design, and neatness of construction, than size and cost," said *Vick's Flower and Vegetable Garden* (1878). What has been forgotten in the twentieth century is that Victorian summerhouses, like Victorian balconies,

porches, and verandas, frequently functioned as trellises for horticultural decoration and were often constructed with a lattice. They were made from wire, milled wood, or branches and twigs in the rustic mode.

**ABOVE:** *There's something romantic about the idea of a garden gate. This one leads to a walled garden.* **OPPOSITE PAGE:** *This is the haughty Gibson Girl, ignoring one of her many would-be beaux.*

## GENTLEMAN'S CHAIR

The gentleman's chair, where the man of the house held court, was the larger of two armchairs appearing in a typical parlor suite.

## GIBSON GIRL

She was beautiful. She was tall and slim. She was modern. She was high-class. The tilt of her head made her appear just a trifle haughty. She was the American ideal. She was the Gibson Girl. Illustrator Charles Dana Gibson introduced his famous Gibson Girl in 1890 in *Life* magazine, and within a few years, she had become a national sensation, her image appearing not only in magazines but on everything from ashtrays to tablecloths. She represented not only a new look for women, but a new role for them, too. The Gibson Girl was just as comfortable on the golf course as she was on the dance floor. (Although she was able to shed a lot of her inhibitions, however, the Gibson Girl was not able to shed her corset.)

## GILBERT & SULLIVAN

Those Victorians who had the means went to the opera to see and to be seen. The fourteen operettas written by Sir William Schwenck Gilbert (1836–1911) and Sir Arthur Seymour Sullivan (1842–1900) between 1871 and 1896 not only kept people going, but kept them laughing, too. People flocked to see *Thespis* (1871); *Trial by Jury* (1875); *The Sorcerer* (1877); *The Pirates of Penzance* (1879); *H.M.S. Pinafore* (1878); *Patience* (1881); *Iolanthe* (1882); *Princess Ida* (1884); *The Mikado* (1885); *Ruddigore* (1887); *The Yeomen of the Guard* (1888); *The Gondoliers* (1889); *Utopia, Limited* (1893); and *The Grand Duke* (1896).

Of these, *The Mikado* and *Patience* are of particular note because they were extremely popular and were satires of life in the nineteenth century. *The Mikado* twitted the era's mania for all things Japonesque, while *Patience* mocked Oscar Wilde and the whole Aesthetic Movement.

In *Patience*, Aesthetic poet Reginald Bunthorne, who looks and acts a lot like Wilde, loves Patience the milkmaid; Patience doesn't like him. After several Aesthetic comic thrusts, the boy-meets-girl theme comes to a surprisingly funny ending. In between, Bunthorne waxes poetic about everything, including his Aestheticism, and declares himself "an Aesthetic sham."

> Am I alone, And unobserved?
> Let me confess!
> A languid love for lilies does *NOT* blight me!
> Lank limbs and haggard cheeks do *NOT*
>   delight me!
> I do *NOT* care for dirty greens
> By any means
> I do *NOT* long for all one sees that's Japanese.

In the end, all is lost—his patience, his Patience, and even his Aesthetic Movement.

## GILDING

Because most people today look at Victorian furnishings in bright sunlight or powerful electric lighting, the common assumption is that Victorians used gilding primarily to make things look elegant and expensive. That was a significant factor, but gilding was also used to enliven the patterns, colors, and shapes of decorative objects when seen at night in the warm and low-level illumination of candles, kerosene lamps, or gaslights. Gold was extensively used on picture frames because it is a neutral color that does not conflict with whatever colors are on the wall, furniture, or work of art. (For similar reasons, seventeenth-century Dutch framers and their imitators in the Aesthetic Movement used black frames.)

## GIRANDOLES

One of the most romantic types of Victorian mantel lighting, girandoles, popular at mid-century, were sets of brass or bronze figural candleholders with marble bases and stunning long glass prisms that reflected and intensified their light. Girandoles were sold in pairs, each of which held a single candle, or in sets of three, which included a centerpiece that had three to five branches. Some designs followed furniture styles, with the bases representing everything from Rococo Revival flower baskets to sinuous grapevines. Others represented figures from history and mythology—everyone from George Washington to Athena, goddess of wisdom.

*In Victorian times, whatever wasn't gold was gilded. Under the glow of gaslight, gilding made picture frames, furniture, and fancy French pier mirrors sparkle like millions of jewels.*

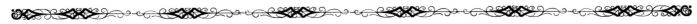

# GLASS DOMES

Wax fruit, hair trees, arrangements of handmade floral displays, and even small stuffed animals and birds were kept under glass domes. The domes protected these objects from the deteriorating effects of dust and dirt and offered an eye-catching way to display prized possessions. Glass domes were equally at home in the parlor, where they could be seen on the center table, étagère, or even the piano.

# GLOVE BUTTON HOOK

One of the attributes of beauty that Victorian women strove for, besides the wasp waist, was the dainty hand. And if the hand was not so small, no matter; a skin-tight leather glove that buttoned up would make it look so, especially if the glove was at least two sizes too small. But how to put it on? This is where the glove hook comes in. The first glove hooks were simple C-shaped hooks of silver or gold; later ones had handles of sterling silver, mother-of-pearl, bone, and ivory. The glove hook was replaced in 1894 by the snap-fastener, and ultimately by the zipper.

# GLOVES

Fashion dictated that women should wear gloves—white, tight-fitting kidskin gloves that were fastened by up to one hundred tiny buttons. Much advice was given not only on buying gloves, but on getting them on. Lillian Russell, that great beauty of the silver screen who made twenty-button, shoulder-length gloves famous, advised allowing at least one half hour to squeeze each hand into the binding leather. (Shopping took much longer, some women spending hours merely trying the gloves on.) After hands were powdered with talcum or a weak solution of alum, a glove stretcher, which bears an uncanny resemblance to the old-fashioned curling iron, was placed in each finger of the glove to expand the leather. By some great miracle—and lots of pushing and pulling and help from the servants—the hand was shoved into the glove. Then a special hook was used to fasten the buttons. Now, all milady had to worry about was not getting the gloves dirty—and, of course, peeling them off.

© John Kosmer

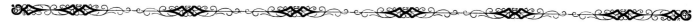

OPPOSITE PAGE, LEFT: *Glass domes filled with wax fruit, flowers, or even stuffed birds were considered chic decorations for the parlor and dining room.* **ABOVE:** *The Gone-With-the-Wind lamp did not appear on the Victorian scene until late in the nineteenth century, but that didn't stop Hollywood from giving it a prominent place in a film about the Civil War. Today, collectors often mistakenly pair such lamps with Rococo Revival furniture from the 1860s.*

# GONE-WITH-THE-WIND LAMP

The lamp that Hollywood gave Rhett and Scarlett as a prop was actually an anachronism. Margaret Mitchell's Civil War soap opera took place in the 1860s and 1870s, but the Gone-With-the-Wind lamp didn't even make its appearance until about 1880, and it didn't go out of style until the 1920s, some two decades before the movie was even made. Although the lamps looked pretty with their matching glass globes of ruby satin or hand-painted or transfer-printed scenes, they didn't give much light. They could, however, be ordered with open student lamp shades, which made them somewhat brighter.

Enormously popular, the lamps, which had center-draft burners, cost from one dollar to five hundred dollars, depending on type and design of the globes. Period catalogs showed up to twenty-five styles each, with the most popular, the ruby satin version, selling for about six dollars. Later versions were made for electric current.

# GOTHIC REVIVAL ARCHITECTURE

When the new Houses of Parliament in London were completed early in the reign of Queen Victoria, the Gothic Revival style was firmly established as Britain's national style. That and subsequent Victorian developments are amply documented in Charles Locke Eastlake's *History of the Gothic Revival* (1872). Surviving examples are more affectionately regarded today than any other variety of Victorian architecture, especially by authors. Late Victorian varieties of medieval styles are now called Ruskinian Gothic and Stick Style. Ruskinian Gothic used the natural colors of various building materials, especially stones and bricks, to create a polychromed Gothic Revival architecture. Stick Style imitated the late medieval folk building of northern Europe, especially its decorative surface patterns. The most popular form of Gothic Revival architecture is

ABOVE: *The so-called Wedding Cake House in Kennebunkport, Maine, is a prime example of a house that was updated during the Victorian period. The original four-square brick house was built in 1826 by George W. Bourne. In 1855, he added the "icing"—the hand-carved pinnacles and Gothic Revival gingerbread.* RIGHT: *Gothic Revival furniture looks like it would be most at home in a church.* OPPOSITE PAGE: *During the Colonial Revival, the idea of putting the grandfather clock in the hallway or on the staircase landing came back into vogue.*

now called Carpenter Gothic—a simplified form characterized by steeply pitched gables and dormers, sometimes with vertical board-and-batten siding, eave trimmings, and pointed-arch windows. In most instances, Carpenter Gothic consisted of the above-mentioned features grafted on a three- or five-bay, central-entrance, neoclassical vernacular, rectangular box. The most famous example is the Wedding Cake House in Kennebunkport, Maine—a neoclassical house built around 1820 and ornamented by a perforated and pinnacled Gothic Revival envelope built around 1845.

## GOTHIC REVIVAL FURNITURE

Victorian furniture that was anything more than merely functional derived its style and public acceptance from literary sources. The Gothic Revival style was energized by the popularity of Sir Walter Scott's novels, and his use of architectural salvage from derelict medieval churches to decorate his residence at Abbotsford in Scotland. Even this endorsement and the early Victorian promotion of the style by A.J. Downing and his associates for their house designs in Gothic Revival styles, however, failed to make it popular. In the United States, the style lacked the symbolic power it had in Britain; it was associated with church architecture, and it looked threatening with its platoons of crockets and pinnacles. The style enjoyed its biggest success in the furnishing of libraries, largely due to the international celebrity of Scott's Gothic Revival library at Abbotsford.

© Nance S. Trueworthy

## GRAINING

To the Victorian eye, looks counted most, and if a home-owner couldn't afford the genuine article, imitation was the sincerest form of flattery. Through the magic of the paintbrush, exterior and interior doors, hallways, kitchens, and pantries were "grained" to resemble more expensive woods like ash, maple, birch, or oak. Although it took a little practice, graining was easy and was done by professionals and amateurs alike. It is a three-step process: applying the base coat and glaze, making the wood grain, and varnishing.

## GRANDFATHER CLOCKS

Yankee ingenuity, in the form of the mass-produced Victorian shelf clock, made the long- or tall-case clock obsolete, but Victorian romanticism rechristened it "grandfather clock" and moved it from its old, functional location in the parlor to its new, symbolic location in the hallway or staircase landing, where it has remained to this day, especially in late Victorian and twentieth-century Colonial Revival homes.

## GRAND TOUR

Travel, in the form of the Grand Tour of Europe, was considered essential to a good education. Ostensibly, these extended trips were made by the well-to-do to soak up culture, but in reality they were an excuse to bring back loads of expensive souvenirs for the parlor, where they would be prominently displayed so as to impress callers. Those who didn't have the means or the time for a months-long Grand Tour could sit back in the comfort of their own humble homes and read travel books like the hilarious Mark Twain spoof *A Tramp Abroad* (1879).

## GREEK SLAVE

Hiram Powers' beautiful marble sculpture of a young, classically undraped maiden whose dainty hands were shackled with chains became one of the most noted pieces of art in the Victorian era, for it showed that the United States was becoming a major player in the art world at a time when Europe was still the leader. The original, larger-than-life *Greek Slave* (1847) was displayed at the Crystal Palace Exhibition in London in 1851 and again at the New York Crystal Palace Exhibition in 1853. If prudish Victorians were shocked by this chastely undressed figure, the acclaim it received at these shows convinced them it was indeed art. By making small, inexpensive parian copies, dealers succeeded in putting a "slave" in every front parlor.

© Randy O'Rourke

**ABOVE:** *The griffin was a fanciful decorative motif used on furniture. Some looked fierce, some looked cutesy; regardless of the griffins' facial expressions, however, the Victorians thought the mythical beasts all looked splendid.* **OPPOSITE PAGE:** *Kate Greenaway was the author of many whimsical and charming designs such as this one.*

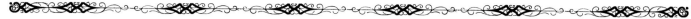

## GREENAWAY, KATE

A celebrated Aesthetic Movement artist, Kate Greenaway (1846–1901) illustrated children's books and had a great influence on children's dress. Up until her time, not much thought had been given to children's clothing—the little ones were simply dressed as miniature adults. Greenaway, taking her cue from the flowing garments of the turn of the previous century, produced not only drawings but actual designs of little girls' ankle-length garments. Like much that was produced in the Aesthetic Movement, however, her designs never caught on with the general public, although they were considered charming.

## GRIFFINS

Wondrous, winged creatures, half eagle, half lion, griffins started appearing on furniture and decorative accessories late in the nineteenth century. They often were depicted in a fierce attitude, with their mouths wide open, and were used as support posts for bookcases or even legs of desks. Cousin to the griffin is the fire-breathing chimera, the ancient Greek she-monster with a lion's head, goat's body, and dragon's or serpent's tail.

## HAIR JEWELRY

Victorians tended to be terribly sentimental when judged by modern standards and clung tenderly to trinkets from dearly departed loved ones. They longed to be connected with these special people, and they found that human hair, which was lightweight, pliable, and tough, could be woven and braided quite nicely into necklaces, bracelets, earrings, and watch chains. Queen Victoria, for instance, couldn't be parted from a bracelet that contained not only a portrait of her dearly departed Albert, but a lock of his hair.

Human hair was not, however, reserved solely for mourning jewelry. Mothers often wove their own hair, placed it inside a special locket that had a glass front, and gave it to their daughters. And young women often presented suitors with similar gifts.

By the 1860s and 1870s, the use of human hair as decoration took on a new dimension. Hair wreaths, or framed floral bouquets made from the locks of several members of the family, were enclosed in glass, framed, and hung in the best parlor for all to see.

Hair even took root in the family tree. The hair of the oldest family members cleverly formed the trunk, while that of the youngest members covered the branches like leaves. The whole ensemble was covered with a glass dome.

# HAIR RECEIVERS

Victorian women were exhorted to brush their long, beautiful tresses at least one hundred times each night, and the strands that remained in the brush were carefully placed into a hair receiver, a small cylindrical container, usually of porcelain, that had a hole in the top. It was one of the many decorations atop the dresser. The precious hair was saved and later woven into hair jewelry or even hairwork pictures and wreaths, encased in glass, that were prominently displayed in the parlor.

# HALL TREE

A staple in the front hall, the hall tree or hall stand was a welcome sight to every guest. It came in a variety of styles and nearly always had a mirror, umbrella stand, and hat rack. Some also had seats with a drawer underneath for storage of shoes and other small items of apparel. Generally, hall stands were massive, while hall trees, which had trunklike centers from which hooks branched out, were smaller, and looked like trees. In smaller houses, the hall tree was merely a hanging mirror in a frame that had several hooks for coats and hats.

# HANDS (DECORATIVE)

Victorians used china, glass, wood, coral, brass, and cast-iron to make elegant female hands, usually having a wrist encircled with a frilled ruff. They were used for door knockers, paper clips, ring holders, calling-card trays, tie-backs, and jewelry. When holding a small vessel, they were used as flower vases and bon-bon dishes.

# HANGING BASKETS

Hanging baskets, or planters, flourish today independent of the Victorian house. During the Victorian period, so many people were tempted to use gorgeous pots, which were usually glazed porcelain or painted and lacked drainage holes, that Edward Sprague Rand's *Flowers for the Parlor and Garden* (1864) had to issue a warning against them and urge the use of common clay pots for their porosity and drainage, adding that the fancy pot "may be used by setting the pot containing the plant inside of [it]." It was unnecessary for Rand to add that wire baskets were to be avoided because the soil in them dried out quickly. Today's plastic hanging baskets are available in colors that imitate terra-cotta and other traditional materials; they can also be painted any color with acrylic paint. "The plants most suitable for a hanging plant," wrote Rand, were common periwinkle (vinca major and minor), *Lysimachia mummularia* (moneywort), *Linaria cymbalaria* (coliseum ivy), *Tradescantia zebrina*, *Careus flagelliformis*, lobelia, nemophila, tropaeolum (nasturtium), *Solanum jasminoides*, *Saxifraga sarmentosa* (Chinese saxifrage), *Convolvulus mauritanicus*, *Pelargonium laterpes* (ivy-leaved geranium),

© Nance S. Trueworthy

**ABOVE:** *The hall tree, which was invariably the first item the guest encountered upon entering the house, was the repository for visitors' hats and wraps, walking canes and parasols, or calling cards (if the mistress was not there to receive the visitors in person).* **OPPOSITE PAGE:** *Victorian verandas and porches are perfect spots to hang baskets of flowers.*

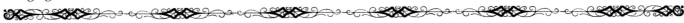

and *Disandra prostata*. In addition to having flowers, an effective Victorian hanging basket depended upon a reliable climber, or trailer. Rand recommended German ivy (*Senecio scandens*); *Vick's Flower and Vegetable Garden* (1878) recommended othonna as a trailer, which "appears to best advantage in a basket when used singly." When hung within the structure of a porch or veranda, baskets should follow the architectural logic of the location and harmonize with its colors.

# HARDY BULBS

"They are, and always will continue to be, popular, on account of their great beauty, and because they require so little labor. No plant, no class of plants, however, possesses all good qualities, and those in this department do not generally keep a flower a long time, as do some of our best annuals and tender bedding plants," stated *Vick's Flower and Vegetable Garden* (1878). Hardy bulbs include hyacinth, crocus, iris, snowdrop, jonquil, narcissus, tulip, lily, tiger flower, *Fritillaria imperialis* (crown imperial), peony, and yucca.

© Karlene V. Schwartz

# HAT PINS

When Victorian women started wearing big, wide-brimmed hats in the 1880s, they needed a way to keep them securely on their heads. Some women tied them under their chins with long scarves; others chose to fasten them with decorative hat pins that came in a variety of styles. The pin itself looks like a lethal weapon—it had to be long and sharp enough to pierce not only the hat but the thick hair of the wearer. Due to the decorative top, it was also a piece of jewelry. In the Montgomery & Ward Co. catalog of 1895, there were eight hat pins, each with a different design. The designs ranged from a silverplated lily for fifteen cents to a sterling sword with intricate hilt for eighty cents. Hat pins were also made out of gold, goldplate, ceramic, glass, wood, shell, and enameled metal.

# HEDGES

Late Victorians would have appreciated the sarcasm of Robert Frost's famous line of poetry about how good fences make good neighbors. "The practice of hedging one's ground so that the passer-by cannot enjoy its beauty, is one of the barbarisms of old gardening," wrote Frank J. Scott in his *Art of Beautifying Suburban Home Grounds* (1870). Scott also counseled not to "plant live hedges on the street fronts of a lawn or suburban residence; but they are very useful and beautiful as separating screens between the decorated ground and the vegetable garden, or as a protection for fruit yards against injurious windows." Plants for hedges recommended by Scott included the arborvitaes, especially "the indigenous American species which is found wild on the banks of the Hudson and other eastern rivers," hemlock, Norway spruce, dwarf species of white pine, and native thorns—especially "the fragrant hawthorn" American holly, wild crab apple, and "the beautiful English hawthorns." Scott condemned the honey locust, because "the labor of restraining their sprouts and suckers is about as profitable as that of training a Bengal tiger to do the work of an ox." For symmetrical clipped hedges viewed on axis, Scott recommended a pyramidal form, with the top clipped to a level surface of six inches, concave sides, and a vertical base six inches in depth. For hedges seen head-on with one side shaded by trees or having a northern exposure, Scott recommended an asymmetrical shape clipped to present a broader surface to compensate for less sunlight on that side.

## HERTER BROTHERS FURNITURE

The most desirable American Aesthetic Movement furniture was made by Herter Brothers in New York City. Gustave Herter, a former silver designer with Tiffany's, founded the firm. After an 1868 apprenticeship in Paris, his younger brother Christian directed the firm to its leadership in progressive furniture of the 1870s and 1880s. Most of the furniture was characterized by Eastlakean rectilinearity, Japonesque ebonized wood, and inlaid flowers in the Japanese lacquer or Dutch marquetry traditions.

*OPPOSITE PAGE: Among the hardy bulbs recommended by* Vick's Flower and Vegetable Garden *was the crocus (in this case* Crocus vernus). **ABOVE:** *This elegant garden in Newport, Rhode Island, features statuary, stone benches, and well-trimmed hedges (to protect the flowers from careless passers-by).* **ABOVE, RIGHT:** *This Egyptian Revival credenza by Herter Brothers displays the sturdy craftsmanship and bold lines typical of their furniture; the center panel features a plaque of "Mitaros, Roi d'Egypt."*

## HIGH SCHOOLS

The transition from rural village to urban town was usually marked by the building of high schools, academies, and normal schools, also called teacher's colleges. They usually appeared in villa and mansion styles, especially the neoclassical Italianate and Mansardic styles. Often they were built at the same time, in the same style, and by the same architect as the town or city hall. State education departments would employ architects to set building standards (e.g., T.H. Burrows, *Pennsylvania School Architecture* [1855], with plans and drawings by "Sloan and Stewart, Architects of the city of Philadelphia"). Many high schools were built after the National Education Act of 1870, but few Victorian high schools survive. The most famous, because it was featured in Alfred Hitchcock's frightening film *The Birds*, was built in 1873 as the Bodega Bay School in California; it is now a restaurant.

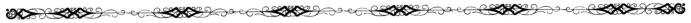

# HOLLAND BULBS AND CAPE BULBS

"Holland Bulbs did not originate in that country, but the good Hollanders have almost monopolized their culture for so many years, doubtless to their own profit and the good of the world, that the name has been conceded, by general consent, to a class of Bulbs, of which the Hyacinth, Tulip and Crocus are the leading members," said *Vick's Flower and Vegetable Garden* (1878). Edward Sprague Rand's *Flowers for the Parlor and Garden* (1864) focused on Cape Bulbs, stating that there was "no finer class of window plants; they are mostly natives of Southern Africa, in the region of the Cape of Good Hope, whence their horticultural name." Rand described ixia, oxalis, babiana, haemanthus (blood flower), amaryllis, lachenalia, sparaxis, anomatheca, tritonia, homeria, and nerine. Rand said *Amaryllis purpurea* is "found in every cottage window," and that "*A. belladina* is the always admired belladona lily." Vick's book said, "The Hyacinth is the most beautiful, and fragrant, and popular of the Holland bulbs, and seems particularly designed for house-culture." Vick completed his listings with colchicum (autumn crocus), galanthus (snowdrop), narcissus (daffodil and jonquil), scilla, anemone, ranunculus, iris, chionodoxa (glory of the snow), and muscarti (grape hyacinth).

# HORN FURNITURE

The horns of Texas longhorns were converted to domestic use in the 1880s by Wenzel Friedrich of San Antonio. Horn furniture was a bizarre twist on the well-established early Victorian tradition of twig or rustic furniture. Friedrich sold armchairs, settees, stools, tables, hall stands, and hat racks made of horns.

# HORSEHAIR UPHOLSTERY

Hairs from horses' tails that didn't find their way into violin bows or crinolines in the Victorian era were used in making an extraordinarily durable upholstery material. In common use, horsehair upholstery was black, unpatterned or monochromatic, and relied on buttoning and tufting for decorative effect.

© John Kosmer

**ABOVE:** *Still a popular upholstery, horsehair was standard in Victorian times. Today there are a variety of colors and patterns, but in the last century black was the big seller. Horsehair tended to be slippery and scratchy.* **OPPOSITE PAGE:** *Horn furniture is mainly associated with Texas, but it was used in other parts of the country as well. Some pieces were made entirely of animal horns. This rustic cabinet, surely one of the more eccentric creations in the genre, is merely decorated with them.*

## HOSPITALS/INSANE ASYLUMS

The traditional function of a mental hospital—as an apartment complex for mentally ill persons—has not changed until relatively recently, while the general hospital has changed dramatically throughout the twentieth century. Old Johns Hopkins Hospital (1877–1885) in Baltimore is a rare, surviving Victorian medical hospital building. Dr. Thomas S. Kirkbride of the Pennsylvania Hospital for the Insane summarized his design philosophy in 1847 in a pamphlet titled *Remarks on the Construction and Arrangements for the Insane*. Kirkbride was a firm believer in the therapeutic Victorian virtues of a building "in good taste to exercise a most favorable influence on many of the insane," situated on a pleasant site with "agreeable scenery," landscaped grounds, and well-ventilated rooms, and located in the countryside with access to a large town. Each ward, he said, should be connected with "a parlour, a dining-room, a clothes-room, a bath-room, a water-closet"—a hospital with all the amenities of a Victorian home. The first hospital designed according to Kirkbride's principles was the New Jersey State Lunatic Asylum, now the Trenton Psychiatric Hospital. Responding to a shocking report by Dorothea Dix in 1844, the New Jersey state legislature authorized the construction of a hospital in 1845, which was completed from the Italianate plans of John Notman in 1848. Its landscape setting was designed by Andrew Jackson Downing. Subsequent asylums were designed in a variety of styles, often achieving the net effect of a classical acropolis, medieval monastery, or Renaissance palace.

## HOTELS: URBAN/SUBURBAN/RESORT

The tradition of the modern urban hotel began in 1828 when Isaiah Rogers designed the Tremont House in Boston. Its innovations, which included indoor plumbing, a lobby, a courtyard, and a magnificent stained-glass skylight, were publicized in a handsome book of 1830 (W.H. Eliot, *A Description of the Tremont House*). Its fate, like most

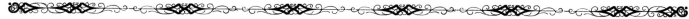

other Victorian urban hotels, was demolition (circa 1895). "In October 1860," writes John Maass, "a young Victorian gentleman told the Mayor of New York that his accommodations at the Fifth Avenue Hotel were more comfortable than his rooms at home. His home was Buckingham Palace, for this was Victoria's son, the Prince of Wales." Suburban hotels, usually built by railroad companies along their commuter routes, survive as small inns or have been converted into boarding schools and apartments. Resort hotels, which functioned as asylums for the mentally weary during "the season," have burned down or fallen down until only a few remain. The most famous survivors are Mohonk Mountain House (1870–1899) near New Paltz, New York, and Hotel Del Coronado (1887–1888) at San Diego. Cape May, New Jersey— the first American seaside resort—has a high percentage of its original resort hotels intact and is still a popular resort area. Saratoga Springs, New York, is as fashionable a summer resort area as it ever was during the Victorian period.

## HOUSE OF WORTH

Charles Frederick Worth, the legendary Paris couturier, clothed well-heeled Victorian women, including Empress Eugenie of France and Empress Elizabeth of Austria, throughout most of the Victorian period. His gowns, made of the most luxurious fabrics and trims, cost thousands of dollars—tremendous sums then and now.

## HUDSON RIVER SCHOOL

Founded by Englishman Thomas Cole (1801–1848), the Hudson River School style of art refers to the grand, and grand-scale, panoramic scenes painted by several artists who took up residence along the Hudson River in New York from the 1820s to the early 1900s. Oddly enough,

this was a distinctly American genre, yet most of the artists, who set up a colony in the old village of Woodstock, were English, or trained in England. The mountainous wilderness along the Hudson River area not only attracted artists, it also attracted tourists. These tourists wanted to remember what they had seen, so they were only too eager to buy prints and lithographs of the scenes painted by the likes of not only Cole but Samuel F.B. Morse, Albert Bierstadt, and Frederic Church.

## HUNZINGER, GEORGE

A German immigrant cabinetmaker, George Hunzinger (1835–1898) lent his name to a series of quirky-looking rockers, chairs, and sofas he patented from the 1860s through the 1890s. Hunzingers are the freaks of the nineteenth-century furniture world, and are definitely an acquired taste. Their machine-inspired, bolt- and coglike decorative elements express the Victorian fascination with the Machine Age. They are highly prized by collectors.

**OPPOSITE PAGE:** *The Victorian era produced some of the grandest of the grand hotels, including the Empress in Victoria, British Columbia, Canada.* **ABOVE:** *This chair is one of Hunzinger's rarer pieces. It is owned by antiques dealer Joan Bogart of Roslyn, New York.*

## INCISING

Used on Renaissance Revival, Aesthetic Movement, and so-called Eastlake furniture, incising is the process of carving simple geometric patterns and stylized floral motifs. The resulting designs were often gilded to highlight them.

## INTERIOR COLORS

Throughout the sixty-three years of Victoria's reign, the style in colors changed several times. Choosing the proper color became a science, and there were all sorts of theories that developed—and then were changed—during the era. Today, because all the colorful vintage fabrics and wallpapers have faded, many people suffer under the mistaken impression that the Victorians liked dull, drab colors. Nothing could be further from the truth; if anything, twentieth-century eyes are likely to find vintage hues glaringly bright. For instance, in choosing the colors for Osborne House in the 1850s, Queen Victoria merely followed Albert and he merely followed the popular style, which favored bright hues. The royal sitting room was pale apple-green, the bedroom was salmon-pink, and the drawing room was blue.

The Victorian enchantment with psychedelic colors and rainbow combinations can be traced to 1856, when ani-line dye was discovered, bringing the purples—magenta, solferino, and Victoria blue—as well as Victoria green and Victoria orange to the world. It wasn't enough, however, to combine these colors; the intensity had to be varied, too. Therefore, to accentuate the contrast, it became chic to show a light and dark color together.

Later, color and even wallpaper styles became connected with the function of the room. Dining rooms were usually crimson, not only in imitation of Sir Walter Scott's Abbotsford but because rich, warm colors were considered aids to digestion and polite conversation. Libraries were painted serious colors (usually dark greens), halls were often painted to look like stone or wood, and parlors were showy and usually bright. Bedrooms, for health reasons, were to be light and devoid of busy, patterned wallpaper, which was likely to frazzle the nerves and disturb slumber.

By the 1870s and 1880s, when the Aesthetic Movement was in full revolt against these bright colors, subdued or even rather dull colors, especially greens, were in vogue. William Morris, although professing that he absolutely hated "dingy bilious yellow-green," usually favored dark green for woodwork, and the colors of the peacock were much advocated not only in interior design but on clothing.

© Richard Sexton

**OPPOSITE PAGE:** *Incising, a late-nineteenth-century technique, was used to bring out the details of furniture. Incised lines were often gilded.* **ABOVE:** *Color theory was a Victorian fetish; it inspired people to assign different colors to different rooms. Scarlets and crimsons, for example, were considered most appropriate in dining rooms because they were thought to aid digestion.*

🌐 **ABOVE:** *This late-nineteenth-century house is a strong example of Italianate architecture. The brackets and bay windows are its most stunning features.* **OPPOSITE PAGE:** *Pieces of Japonesque transfer-printed earthenware were executed in monochrome and polychrome.*

## INVENTIONS

The Victorians came up with all sorts of scientific and technological advances, many of which drastically changed their lives. Along with more useful inventions like the airplane, light bulb, telephone, telegraph, typewriter, sewing machine, and gramophone, the nineteenth century ushered in a whole host of more frivolous items, including a ship on wheels, an automatic page turner, an automatic scent dispenser, a talking watch, and a picture book that made animal noises.

## ITALIANATE ARCHITECTURE

Victorian revivals of Italian Renaissance architecture took several forms, from America's first Florentine palazzo, designed by John Notman for The Athenaeum of Philadelphia (1845–1847), to stacks of cast-iron arcades-within-colonnades for commercial districts before and after the Civil War, to Riverside (1839), America's first picturesque villa on the British Regency model, designed by Notman for an eccentric Episcopalian bishop named George Eashington Doane at Burlington, New Jersey, to the bracketed rectangular and square boxes, often with campanile towers and belvedere observatories, that replaced Greek Revival–style houses as America's most popular home style in the 1850s. During the rapid growth of the Midwest and West, the popularity of Italianate architecture was aided by its adaptability to the simplified construction technique of balloon framing (invented in Chicago in 1832) and by the proliferation of mass-produced architectural details sold nationally through millwork catalogs. The most common Italianate house was built on an L-plan, now called a Homestead House or Tri-Gabled El House. It was closely followed in popularity by the hipped-roof Square House. Both types survived in North America until the First World War.

## JAPONESQUE TRANSFER-PRINTED EARTHENWARE

After the 1876 Centennial Exhibition, when everyone had a yen for everything that was Japanese, the English started producing sets of dishes decorated with Japonesque-motif transfer prints. Leading manufacturers, including Minton and Co., created various designs in monochrome and polychrome not only for sale at home in England, but for export to the United States.

# JAPONISME

*Japonisme* is a French word that refers to the Japan craze that swept the West after Commodore Matthew C. Perry opened trade with that country in 1854. Because Japan had been so isolated, it took a long time, even after Perry's expedition, before its art became generally known to the outside world. In fact, it was not until the 1876 Centennial Exhibition, where Japan had a stunning display, that the craze caught on.

The craving for everything Japanese took many forms. Not only did the Victorians want genuine Japanese objects and products, which were considered extremely exotic, they also wanted to make their own versions. The top artists of the West incorporated Oriental motifs—fans, cranes, storks, owls, wild carp, bamboo trees, cherry trees, and even Mount Fuji—into their designs for architecture, furniture, ceramics, wallpapers, fabrics, lighting, book covers, clocks, silver vases, flatware and tea sets, door handles and escutcheons, jewelry, screens, and crazy quilts. In addition, they began creating works in cloisonne and lacquer. By the time these artists were finished borrowing motifs, the finished object looked more American than Japanese

Although most people simply bought a paper fan or parasol and placed it artistically in the front parlor, some wealthy individuals filled their mansions with faux bamboo and ebonized furniture, and decorative accessories in the Japonesque style. At least one person—designer-architect Harvey Ellis—took to wearing silk kimonos. Gilbert & Sullivan's *Mikado* satirized the craze.

*(photo credit, rotated: © Richard Sexton)*

**ABOVE:** *Everyone who attended the Centennial Exposition in 1876 was taken by the Japanese display. Soon, Japonesque furnishings, notably bamboo or faux bamboo chairs and étagères, along with various pieces of bric-a-brac, found their way into the Victorian home. Although few had the means or the design expertise to carry the theme throughout a room or an entire house, a Japonesque fan was usually enough to get the idea across.* **OPPOSITE PAGE:** *In the 1980s, the kaleidoscope, the Victorian version of the video game, enjoyed a renaissance. Today, there are many styles—old and new—from which to choose.*

# JELLIFF, JOHN J.

Furnituremaker John J. Jelliff (1813–1893) set up shop in Newark, New Jersey, in the 1840s. Although his firm followed the furniture styles of the day, he is best known for his Renaissance Revival pieces. He was forced by ill health to retire in 1860, but the business continued. The Newark Museum has an excellent collection of Jelliff furniture.

# JET JEWELRY

Popular during the latter part of the nineteenth century, jet jewelry was mourning jewelry made of highly polished coal mined on the Yorkshire coast of England, especially in Whitby. On display at the Crystal Palace Exhibition in 1851, it became even more popular after Prince Albert's death in 1861. By the 1880s, jet jewelry had fallen from favor. Jet is often confused with the French imitation of shiny purple-black glass beads.

# K

## KARPEN BROTHERS FURNITURE

Founded in 1880 by Solomon Karpen and his seven brothers, the Chicago firm of Karpen Brothers was known for its moderately priced furniture in all styles from Colonial Revival to Art Nouveau. Although the company won the 1904 St. Louis World's Fair grand prize for upholstered furniture for a sinuous six-piece Art Nouveau parlor suite, much of its furniture was considered uninspired, and pieces were often an odd conglomeration of styles.

## KALEIDOSCOPE

This Victorian bauble was invented in 1816 by Scottish scientist Sir David Brewster when he put some angled mirrors and some glass beads into a tube and held it up to the light. The images produced by the kaleidoscope so dazzled the public that some 200,000 of the ocular instruments were snapped up in Europe within a matter of months. Although it was close to the turn of the century before Charles Bush of Boston created an American version, the kaleidoscope became an instant success and was the quintessential parlor accoutrement. Today, the form is undergoing a renaissance, and new scopes are as pretty to look at as they are to look into.

## KASHMIR SHAWL

It was its Oriental palm or pine design that made the Kashmir shawl an extremely appealing and exotic piece of apparel from the early 1800s up to about 1870. Hand-woven in Kashmir, India, from the soft wool of the Tibetan goat, these shawls were terribly expensive, even by today's standards. With genuine ones reportedly going for about five hundred to five thousand dollars, they were such status symbols that some women even preferred them to diamonds.

## KEROSENE LIGHTING

One of the great Victorian developments in artificial illumination, kerosene lighting quickly became the people's light after petroleum was discovered in Pennsylvania in 1859. Despite efforts by major manufacturers of kerosene lamps, such as Fietz in New York and Cornelius in Philadelphia, to market fancy parlor lamps and ballroom chandeliers in Rococo, Gothic, and Classical revival styles, the vast majority of kerosene lamps were cheap, vulgar, and utilitarian. These cheap lamps were rarely ugly, but they are ignored today in favor of the fancy lamps. Nonetheless, these lamps are among the few remaining economical

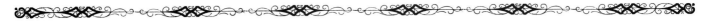

© John Kosmer

## KITCHEN GARDENS

Andrew Jackson Downing rhapsodized about home-grown vegetables in "A Chat in the Kitchen Garden" in the October 1849 issue of his *Horticulturalist*, but twenty years later Frank J. Scott was making fun of them in his *Art of Beautifying Suburban Home Grounds* (1870). A business-man responded to his dinner guest's compliments on the corn. "'I'm glad you appreciate it,' said he; 'it is from my own grounds, and I find that the season's crop will cost me only ten dollars an ear.'" In those twenty years the United States shifted from a rural nation to an urban nation, and with it homegrown vegetables changed from a village necessity to a suburban luxury. That is why early Victorian kitchen gardens were exposed in the landscape and late Victorian kitchen gardens were screened.

## KNICKERBOCKERS

More commonly called knickers, these loose trousers that ended in a buckled band just below the knee were developed in the 1850s. They were considered sportswear.

## KUGELS

Heavy glass Christmas tree ornaments, kugels were made in Germany, starting in the middle of the Victorian era. The earlier kugels, the most desired by collectors, are hand-blown; later ones were blown into molds. The ornaments, which were silvered and often decorated with hand-painted designs and glitter, were usually round, oval, or shaped like big bunches of grapes. Although silver was the most common color, kugels were produced in golds, reds, greens, and blues.

ways to re-create an authentically Victorian interior. Although cheap lamps were shown in catalogs without shades, Dietz and others sold sheets of thick paper printed in colors with elaborate landscapes and other pictures—sometimes with three-dimensional parts—that could be cut out at home and made into paper lamp shades.

## KICKSHAW

A fancy name for a side dish or relish, a kickshaw could be fare as simple and as obvious as stalks of fresh celery, pickles, or ketchup or as complicated as deviled sardines. Many kickshaws, like the celery and sardines, were considered exotic foods at the time and, as such, were displayed in special dishes.

© Dency Kane

**OPPOSITE PAGE:** *Kerosene lamps were a vast improvement over candlelight, but they produced their own set of problems.* **ABOVE:** *This kitchen garden is thriving under the watchful eye of a scarecrow.*

## LACE

Victorian women used lace to dress their rooms as well as themselves. Lace was used as fringe ornamentation for the borders of fine textile furnishings and clothing. The triumph of machine-made lace was made possible by the invention of the lace curtain machine in the 1840s by John Livesey; manufactured lace bed and table coverings followed. Nottingham, England, was the most famous center of such products. (Nottingham lace is still being made.) The best Victorian illustrations are in the catalogs of the International Exhibitions held in Chicago, Dublin, London, New York, Paris, Philadelphia, and Vienna.

## LADY'S CHAIR

Part of the typical parlor suite, the lady's chair was the smaller companion of the gentleman's armchair. It saved many a woman in distress from her dress—hoopskirts, for instance, were known to fly up in the face when one sat down. To accommodate the changing fashion of the day, the lady's chair was modified as the bustle and hoopskirt came into vogue. Usually lower and narrower than the gentleman's chair, it was the only sensible place for the woman of the house to sit.

## LAMBREQUIN

*Lambrequin* is a fancy French word for an even fancier valance, and was often mispronounced as "lamberkin." Later, it also came to mean every shaped pendant of cloth, whether it was on a mantel, a shelf, or a table. In *American Woman's Home* (1869), Catherine E. Beecher and Harriet Beecher Stowe gave instructions for making a lambrequin of chintz, suggesting that it "be embellished with white muslin curtains" and "trimmed with fringe or gimp… a tassel at the lowest point improves the appearance." For those who weren't or didn't have to be handy with a needle and thread, Bloomingdale's Illustrated 1886 Catalog offered three mantel lambrequins, each two and a half feet long and embroidered and trimmed.

**OPPOSITE PAGE:** *This late-nineteenth-century half-tester brass bed is lavishly shrouded in lace. Despite the lacy stereotype, most Victorians did not use lace to this extent, particularly around the bed. Victorians had some strange ideas about bedrooms, believing that heavy bed clothes were most injurious to good health.* **LEFT:** *The armless chair was designed to accommodate some of the more voluminous and unwieldy styles of women's clothing that proliferated during the nineteenth century.*

# LANGUAGE OF FLOWERS

In the "poetical introduction" to her *Flora's Lexicon* (1839), Catharine Waterman said, "There is a language in each flower/That opens to the eye,/A voiceless—but a magic power." Such collections of poetry and sentiment, often illustrated with colored lithographs and handsomely bound, were a staple of early Victorian publishing. The symbolic association of sentiments with flowers was an ancient practice, but the Victorians collected and packaged flower lexicons in what were essentially encyclopedias. The extent to which Victorians used this "language" to send messages is debatable. To ensure that the flowers sent conveyed comprehensible messages, it was necessary for sender and receiver to use the same book, because the lexicon varied from one volume to another. Such books usually had two indexes in the back—a flower index for the recipient and an interpretation index for the sender. The majority of books featuring floral sentiments were not intended for the conveyance of coded messages, but rather as pleasant journeys into the poetry of flowers. Perhaps the best way to use such a volume today is as a romantic dictionary of Victorian emotions.

# LAVA JEWELRY

One of the souvenirs that travelers who took the Grand Tour brought back with them was lava jewelry from Pompeii. In white, beige, olive, gray, or chocolate, the lava was usually carved into classical medallions that resembled cameos. Usually mounted in metal, lava jewelry was popular starting around 1850.

# LAWNS

"These two things," wrote Frank J. Scott in *Art of Beautifying Suburban Home Grounds* (1870), "are the most essential to the businessman's house—a fine lawn and large trees." In the recommended seed mixtures, Scott wisely avoids monoculture. One is composed of equal parts by weight of Kentucky bluegrass, redtop, and white clover seed. The other has twelve quarts Rhode Island bent grass, four quarts creeping bent grass, ten quarts redtop, three quarts sweet vernal grass, two quarts Kentucky bluegrass, and one quart white clover. Scott also wisely focuses on the practical problem of mowing the lawn. "Places that are so cluttered with flowers, trees, and shrubs that it becomes a vexatious labor for a good mower to get in among them, are certainly not well planted."

# LIBRARY FURNISHINGS

At a time when a man's house was his castle, the library was his private domain and inner sanctum. It was in the library that he kept his books and important papers, and it was to the library that he retired alone to smoke and think, sometimes in the company of gentlemen dinner guests. And it was to the library that young gentlemen callers went with great trepidation to ask for a daughter's hand in marriage.

The library's decor was considered masculine and followed the lead of Sir Walter Scott, who decorated Abbotsford in general—and his library in particular—in the Gothic Revival style. Gothic bookcases filled with the latest volumes covered most of the walls and soared almost to the ceiling. (Never mind that many nouveaux riches never read them—lots of books looked good, nevertheless.) A Gothic desk usually dominated the room, whose walls were often paneled or mocked Scott's faux-stone and faux-English oak walls.

The library was supposed to be a serious room and colors were to be grave, even severe. Dark green was the suggested color. Since this was also to be a learned-looking room, plaster or marble busts of Shakespeare and Dante or other suitable luminaries were often seen perched on ornamental brackets.

At least one man of the house, though, did not use the library in the conventional way. Mark Twain's library was not tucked away in the inner bowels of his Hartford, Connecticut, mansion; it was on the ground floor and included a conservatory. In the Twain library, with its massive Scottish mantelpiece, the bookcases, which go only halfway up the walls, ring the room. Actually, it was more

of a family room, where Twain told his little daughters funny stories—the girls made him include all the decorations on the mantel in the plots—and where the children put on plays and other entertainments.

Where did Mr. Twain work and entertain his cronies? In the upstairs billiard room, where he was just barely able to fit a desk next to the all-encompassing pool table and a big Bible that shows no signs of ever having been opened.

## LIGHTHOUSES

Lighthouses were impressive technical achievements of optical and building technology, as well as some of the most impressive architectural ornaments of Victorian coastlines. Although electric lights and radar have rendered most of them obsolete today, many lighthouses survive as popular tourist attractions and are used, in the Victorian manner, for "taking the prospect."

**OPPOSITE PAGE:** *There were many versions of "the language of flowers," and all of them assigned different meanings to each bloom.* **ABOVE, LEFT:** *Libraries generally were masculine domains, but this one belonged to a woman, English writer Vita Sackville-West.* **ABOVE:** *Lighthouses were not just monuments; they were concrete testimonials to the advances of science.*

# LINCRUSTA

One of the alternatives to wallpaper, Lincrusta is a thick, heavily embossed material that is still sold today. In 1877, the Englishman Frederick Walton patented the process of embossing semiliquid linseed oil that was backed with waterproof paper or heavy canvas. About five years later Lincrusta was being made commercially. Lincrusta, which looked a lot like linoleum and was practically indestructible, was an extremely versatile wall surface because it could be painted, stained, gilded, glazed, or even grained. Homeowners who could not afford to hang embossed leathers, woods, or metals on the walls opted for Lincrusta. It was particularly appropriate for dining rooms and front halls because its surface was easy to keep clean.

# LITHOPHANES

Lithophanes were translucent porcelain panels made in a mold, the thickness of which could be manipulated to create subtle images that appeared to have been painted in grisaille. Since their magic was visible only when light was transmitted through them, lithophanes were popular for early Victorian lighting fixtures.

# LITTLE LORD FAUNTLEROY SUITS

"Costume" is the right word to describe this little-boy getup that appeared near the end of the century. More romantic than practical, the garb—a velvet tunic that ended just below the waist, tight knickerbockers, a long wide bow at the neck, and a wide, white-lace collar and matching cuffs—was inspired by the story of the same name. But as more than one little boy undoubtedly learned, clothes do not a Little Lord Fauntleroy make unless, of course, he has the long, curly locks to carry off the look. And even then, the look never became terribly popular and the few who were forced to wear such suits were considered sissies.

# LOVESEAT

A smaller version of the sofa, a loveseat was about three to five feet long and its seat was lower than that of a sofa, about fourteen to fifteen inches from the floor. The loveseat was usually sold as part of a parlor set and was much more romantic than a sofa, because its very construction forced courting couples to sit close together.

**ABOVE:** *The loveseat (in this case, upholstered with tufted and buttoned damask) was designed to bring the trembling knees of a courting couple into intimate (and acceptable) contact.* **OPPOSITE PAGE:** *The chandelier in this dining room has been graced with the addition of light-diffusing pendants, and is therefore a lustre; enhanced light sources such as this one lend undeniable charm and warmth to any room.*

© Brian Vanden Brink

## MAGIC LANTERNS

Long before there were movies, with or without sound, there were magic lanterns. These mysterious boxes that projected images from a tiny slide onto a big screen were invented in the seventeenth century. By Victorian times, the industry was flourishing. Although the magic lanterns themselves were quite decorative—one version was even mounted atop a glass oil lamp—it was the beautifully colored glass slides that were most enchanting. In 1895, the Montgomery Ward & Co. catalog carried several types of magic lanterns from the modest Gloria lantern that created a two-foot picture to the New York Model Sciopticon "for Sunday schools, societies, Army posts, home and public entertainment." There was also a toy magic lantern that had "plain slides highly colored for amateurs." Although this toy version had several slide subjects from which to choose—nursery rhymes, Mother Goose fables, American and German scenery, and world's fairs—special orders, the catalog duly noted, were not taken.

One of the most popular series of slides ever produced was "'Twas the Night Before Christmas," and at the holidays Mama, Papa, and all the little ones would gather around the magic lantern to see the pretty pictures.

## LUSTRES

When a lamp, candleholder, or chandelier was decorated with cut-glass prisms, it was given the fanciful name "lustre" because of the way it shone when lighted. The easiest way to make a lamp or fixture sparkle was to add prisms, which came in a variety of cuts. This was an inexpensive way to update lighting fixtures; consequently, many people used these enhanced lights.

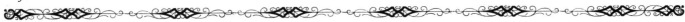
# MAJOLICA

Originally a tin-glazed earthenware, majolica during the Victorian era began to include all earthenwares decorated with semitransparent colored glazes. Minton and Co. displayed a collection of majolica at the 1851 London Crystal Palace Exhibition that imitated original Italian Renaissance designs. Subsequently, a number of potteries in Europe and the United States made majolica bric-a-brac decorated with gaudy colors and designs depicting various naturalistic images. Late Victorian whatnots and plate rails were polychromed with majolica. It was also used for more mundane wares, such as flower pots, plant stands, vases, and umbrella stands.

**ABOVE:** *Majolica was considered garish and without class. Today, however, it brings high prices from collectors. Reproductions of many of the simpler pieces are available.* **ABOVE, RIGHT:** *Stylish Victorian women didn't use much makeup, but what little that was deemed proper was kept in pretty cut-glass scent and powder bottles on their dressers.* **OPPOSITE PAGE:** *The dominant feature of this house is its mansard roof.*

# MAKEUP

In Louisa May Alcott's classic primer on morality, *An Old-Fashioned Girl* (1870), Fanny is asked by her brother, Tom, if his fiancée, a lady of questionable taste and values, "paints." She pretends to misunderstand the question and teasingly replies, "Yes, and draws, too." Tom persists, saying he believes she paints her face because she won't let him kiss her on the cheek but will only allow a slight peck on the lips. "Painting," which good-girl Polly, the old-fashioned heroine, would never do, was considered vulgar during the crinoline and bustle eras. Polly proved she didn't have to do it to win Tom, who eventually saw that her unpainted face was the one for him. While rouge and paint were no-nos, beauty soaps, face creams, and even rice powders and the slightest bit of scent were acceptable later in the era. As always, however, fashion dictated some pretty scary treatments: to keep their lily-white complexions, for instance, women used to eat arsenic!

## MANSARDIC ARCHITECTURE

The rebuilding of Paris under the direction of George Eugene Haussman during the 1850s and 1860s, just prior to the swift defeat of France in the Franco-Prussian War of 1870, was the most famous Victorian urban renewal project. It revived the baroque architecture of Louis XIV in such projects as the enlargement of the Louvre (1852–1857) and featured a double-pitched roof associated with a seventeenth-century royal architect named Mansart—hence this architecture is now called Second Empire or Mansardic. American stylebooks and patternbooks regarded the style as one featuring richly decorated details and a dormered living space in the attic created by what they called "a French roof." Major surviving examples are James Renwick's Corcoran Gallery (1859–1861) in Washington, now the Renwick Gallery; Alfred B. Mullet's State, War, and Navy Building (1871–1888) in Washington; W.W. Boyington's Terrace Hill (1867–1869) in Des Moines, now the Iowa Governor's Mansion; and the city halls of Boston, Baltimore, and Philadelphia. Mansardic buildings like these, which captured the opulence of Napoleon III's Second Empire (1852–1870), were rare; most consisted of

French hats on Italianate bodies. Mansardic was the high Victorian phase of neoclassicism, which began in early Victorian Greek Revival and its ornamentalized cousin, Italianate, and ended in the pomposities of late Victorian Beaux Arts classicism.

## MANSION-STYLE ARCHITECTURE

Americans have been only slightly less uncomfortable with the class-conscious term "mansion" than with "castle." Hence the cute use of "cottage" to describe colossal summer palaces of the late Victorian plutocracy at Newport, Rhode Island, such as Richard Morris Hunt's The Breakers, completed in 1895 for Cornelius Vanderbilt. Hunt also designed a mansion in the French château style for Mrs. William K. Vanderbilt at 660 Fifth Avenue in New York City, but most Victorian mansions were "country houses," a euphemism developed after the Civil War and still in use. It refers to a masonry structure of palatial proportions picturesquely sited in the midst of a large estate. Any historic style, with the exception of Egyptian Revival, had the potential for mansions, but the success of most Victorian architects in this department was in direct proportion to their emulation of a historic palace, palazzo, castle, chateau, or monastery.

## MANTEL CLOCKS

Early Victorian parlors were distinguishable from late Victorian ones by what was put on the fireplace mantel. Early Victorian mantels often featured girandoles. Late Victorian mantels often featured a mantel clock of cast white-metal (cast-iron painted to look like lacquer or marble), brass, or marble. Sometimes they were flanked by fancy candelabra, statues, or fine porcelains, according to the style of the parlor.

© Robert Perron

▨ **ABOVE:** *A clock was only one of the many decorations used on mantels. This mantelpiece has an overmantel that is highly detailed. The fireplace itself is surrounded by art tiles, which were popular late in the century.* **OPPOSITE PAGE:** *This rosewood meridienne, or recamier, is a romantic-looking piece of furniture. Executed in the Rococo Revival style, this item would have been at the height of popularity right before the Civil War.*

## MARBLE

White and red marble were used as tops for Rococo Revival and Renaissance Revival dressers, center tables, and étagères. Most often, the marble was set atop the wooden frame, but on occasion it was inset, framed by the wood of the furniture. It not only gave depth, color, and texture to the furniture, it diminished the massiveness of many of the pieces. Marble cracks and breaks easily, so many of the original tops have not survived. Pieces with original marble usually sell for more than those with replacement tops.

## MARBLEIZING

In the early part of the nineteenth century, marbleizing, a technique of painting areas like fireplace mantels and hallway walls to imitate the more expensive marble, was considered quite desirable. As time went on, however, and design reformers reared their tasteful heads, such mimicry was considered not only unattractive but dishonest and gaudy. Marbleizing was a good project for the do-it-yourselfer.

## MEEKS, J. & J.W.

John and Joseph W. Meeks, who came from a family of furniture makers, were one of John Henry Belter's main competitors in the Rococo Revival style in the 1850s. Belter pieces are considered more delicate and intricate, and superior overall. Recognizable Meeks' patterns include "Stanton Hall," "Henry Ford," and "Hawkins," which were named for the estates they came from. The firm closed in 1868.

## MERIDIENNE/RECAMIER

A short sofa or one-sided lounge in the Rococo Revival style that looks like an elongated one-arm chair, the meridienne (also called a recamier) often came in pairs that were made to face each other.

## MORRIS CHAIR

One of the great ironies of Victorian decorative arts terminology is the naming of an adjustable-backed, wood-frame chair with spindles under the padded arms and a loose-cushioned back and seat for William Morris. Although it was sold by his late Victorian decorative furnishing company, he didn't invent the form, which was derived from the folk vernacular Suffolk chair.

## MORRIS, WILLIAM

During his own time, William Morris (1834–1896) was known as a poet and socialist who also happened to design furniture, tapestries, tiles, stained glass, carpets, textiles, wallpapers, and illuminated books in a quasi-medieval style. Today, however, his contributions to the decorative arts are remembered and applauded.

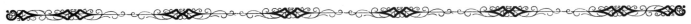

Morris, who had a degree in theology from Oxford, was a Renaissance man. He painted and apprenticed briefly with an architect and was well-established as a writer of romantic verse and medieval-style tales. His best-known works include *News from Nowhere* and the four-volume Chaucer-style tale *The Earthly Paradise*. At age forty-nine, he became a socialist and added political tracts to his repertoire.

Considered the father of the Arts & Crafts Movement, Morris and his friends Dante Gabriel Rossetti, Edward Burne-Jones, Ford Maddox Brown, and Philip Webb formed an interior decorating company in 1861. They focused on the designs of medieval times, when hand-crafting techniques were at their peak. (Incidentally, Morris' furniture, which had art panels by the pre-Raphaelites, brought the latter's work to a wider audience.)

By the 1870s, Morris was designing wallpapers, using a set of naturalistic motifs. "Willow Bough," "Daisy," "Chrysanthemum," and "Pomegranate" are some of the better-known designs. His most memorable fabric is "Strawberry Thief," which depicts a bird stealing berries. And the "Kelmscott Chaucer," a beautifully illuminated version of the *Canterbury Tales*, is considered a masterpiece.

Courtesy of Bradbury & Bradbury

Because Morris' products were so expensive, they never achieved the great popularity the designer had hoped for. He was also personally unhappy. Morris' stunningly beautiful wife, Jane Morris, who often modeled for pre-Raphaelite painters, had a years-long public affair with Rossetti.

## MOURNING

In 1861, the unfortunate Queen Victoria lost both her mother and her beloved husband, Albert, whom she considered the light of her life. Society decreed that widows be in deep mourning for a year after the death and not appear in public unless their faces were covered up and their bodies were shrouded in black. After that followed a period of "second" or "half-mourning" in which they were allowed to wear charcoal grays. Then, as time passed, widows could slip into ever-lightening colors like violet and, finally, heliotrope. Only then could they return to the world of life and color. In the meantime, everything was bordered by black. Mourning customs persisted throughout the nineteenth century, and by 1895 black-bordered handkerchiefs were still being offered in the Montgomery & Ward Co. catalog, as were mourning papeteries that had "superfine cream wove, smooth finish, ruled octavo mourning border and baronial envelopes to match."

Victoria's grief, however, lasted her entire life, and so did her widow's weeds. When she wasn't in seclusion, she was going about dedicating memorials to Albert. The effect was twofold: other society widows followed her example, giving a big boost to the crepe trade, and all the official memorials spawned a profusion of home decorations (among them wax crosses and harps and anchors adorned with wax flowers), to honor a host of less princely personages taken by death.

## NAPKIN FOLDING

Napkin folding became an art during the Victorian era and was a nice way to set off each place at the table besides. Sometimes, bread was folded into the napkin; at other times elaborate, almost origami-like patterns were created.

**OPPOSITE PAGE:** *This reproduction Victorian bedroom features wallpapers based on the designs of the eminently talented William Morris.* **ABOVE:** *Napkin folding was an art that the properly set dinner table featured to advantage; the use of napkin rings in this setting suggests that the meal will be a family affair.*

## NAPKIN RINGS

Despite their fanciful shapes and romantic appeal, napkin rings had a real utilitarian function: they served as a handy identification marker so the same diner could use the same napkin several times before laundering it. Napkin rings were used at family meals but never at dinner parties.

## NEEDLEWORK TOOLS AND ACCESSORIES

The person who first put an eye in a needlelike fragment of bone and used it to sew something probably created the most important invention in human history. All needlework tools and containers are important cultural documents; all are eminently collectible; and many, including those of the Victorian period, are quite decorative. Unlike modern practice, which segregates utilitarian needlework in a "sewing room," Victorian needlework was always pursued in public, and both the tools and the finished pieces were often elegantly stored in special cases, boxes, drawers, and tables.

## NEWEL POST

The central stairway was a prime decorative element in the Victorian house, and the newel post, the principal post or pillar that stood at its foot, was its most impressive point. The newel post was fancier than the other balusters and invariably had a rounded finial that made it easy to grasp when ascending or descending the stairs. Grand staircases had two matching newel posts. The 1897 catalog of Young & Marten in London shows an array of twenty-five newel posts, available in pine, oak, mahogany, or walnut. French polishing cost a little extra.

# NEWEL POST LIGHT

If the newel post of the central stairway did not have a finial, chances are it had a light. These lights were usually figural statues that held some type of torch over their heads. The Mitchell, Vance & Co. catalog, circa 1876, shows gas newel post fixtures thirty-six inches to sixty-six inches in height. There were goddesses, American Indians, warriors, knights, and musketeers, all balancing etched globes. Most held one light; some held up to five.

# NIGHT BLOOMERS

One has to imagine that there just weren't many excuses for staying up late for the hardworking Victorians because one of their favorite pastimes was watching night bloomers, cacti that open their flowers when all the lights are out. Relatives, friends, and neighbors would gather—all dressed up, no less—around the parlor table for the midnight shows. Indeed, the Staten Island Historical Society even has a photo taken in 1890 by Alice Austen that shows the showy blooms of a night-blooming cereus and all the people watching the show.

# NURSERY PAPERS

Up until the Victorian era, children had been treated as little adults. They were dressed just like their parents, and their rooms were furnished with children's furniture, miniature versions of what was in the rest of the house. This attitude started to change around mid-century, and it was then that wallpapers designed specifically for the nursery came into being.

The first artist-designed nursery paper, Walter Crane's "Nursery Rhymes," didn't appear, however, until 1876. "Nursery Rhymes" illustrated all the common children's stories like "Humpty Dumpty." Crane's "Ye Frog He Would A-Wooing Go," which is in the Mark Twain Memorial in Hartford, Connecticut, is also well known. "The Sleeping Beauty," also by Crane, is intriguing not because of its snoozing cats, dogs, and peacocks, but because the reclining beauty is rather skimpily clad.

As the twentieth century opened, other noted artists, including Kate Greenaway and Beatrix Potter, also designed wallpapers for the nursery.

**OPPOSITE PAGE:** *The newel post was made to match the woodwork not only on the central stairway but also on the doorways. Here, the rounded newel post echoes the grand archway of the entrance hall.* **ABOVE:** *Although the newel post light did provide extra illumination, there was a snob factor involved: it showed that the homeowner had good taste — and deep pockets.*

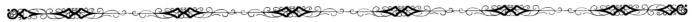

## OBSERVATORIES: BELVEDERES/ TOWERS/CUPOLAS

The rooflines of many Victorian villas and mansions, especially those in the Italianate and Mansardic styles, were rendered more picturesque with the addition of elevated areas for observing the surrounding landscape. Hence the use of the Italian word for "beautiful view," *belvedere*, to describe such structures. With the installation of a telescope, belvederes became true observatories. They often were placed on the uppermost ridge of the apex of the highest-hipped roof.

They could be rectangular, square, octagonal, hexagonal, or circular and were roofed in a variety of ways to conclude their vertical thrusts. "Cupola" properly refers to the underside of a domed space, but it was loosely applied to any observatory located on the center of a building. The sole function of most towers and turrets, located at various positions on the perimeter of a building, was to provide elevated rooms for "taking the prospect."

## OCTAGON BUILDINGS

The octagonal-building plan, like many central-plan structures, has been used for monumental purposes at various times in history, but not for domestic purposes until Orson Square Fowler, a practitioner of the popular Victorian "science" called phrenology by its friends and bump-reading by its enemies, promoted it in his *A Home For All* (1848). The most spectacular surviving examples are Samuel Sloan's design for Longwood (1855) near Natchez, Mississippi, which was left unfinished in 1861 due to the outbreak of the Civil War, and the Arnmour-Steiner House near Irvington, New York (1860), which received an extravagant octagonal dome and observatory in 1872.

## OFFICE BUILDINGS

Tall, late Victorian office buildings, better known today as "skyscrapers," have a large fan club because they are the most obvious link between nineteenth- and twentieth-century cities. Major developments took place in Chicago, hence the importance of what is now called The Chicago School of Architecture and its star attractions: William LeBaron Jenny's Home Life Building (1883–1885), the first to be constructed with a completely iron-and-steel skeleton; the Reliance Building (1890) by Burnham and Root; and others by Holabird and Roche or Adler and Sullivan.

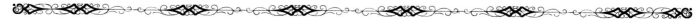

© Balthazar Korab

[▨] **OPPOSITE PAGE:** *Towers allowed Victorians to take a vast view of the countryside.* **ABOVE:** *Orson Fowler was the chief proponent of the octagonal house.*

## OHR, GEORGE

Called the "mad potter of Biloxi," George Edgar Ohr (1857–1918) did everything he possibly could to live up to the image. His Arts & Crafts pieces, created between 1880 and 1910, were weird by any and all standards. Using local Mississippi clay, Ohr crafted paper-thin pieces that he twisted into eccentric shapes, then covered them with what at the time were considered bizarre glazes. His contemporaries didn't appreciate Ohr's pottery, but the thousands of unsold pieces he stockpiled are now worth a fortune, just as he had said they would be.

## ORCHARDS AND ESPALIERS

Andrew Jackson Downing is famous for books on Victorian landscape gardening and rural architecture, but his most successful book was *Fruits and Fruit-Trees of America* (1845). "Fine fruit is the flower of commodities," quoted Downing in the preface. "It is the most perfect union of the useful and the beautiful that the earth knows. Trees full of soft foliage; blossoms fresh with spring beauty; and finally,—fruit, rich, bloom-dusted, melting, and luscious,— such are the treasures of the orchard. He who owns land and only raises crabs and choke-pears, deserves to lose the respect of all sensible men." Dwarf and semidwarf fruit trees expand the variety that can be planted in a small orchard—as many as one hundred in one half-acre, according to an article by Jack Cook. For homes without yards, fruits can be espaliered against walled gardens, but the plantings take a long time to mature. Victorians achieved quicker results with the "oblique cordon" technique, which involved planting young, single-stem trees at eighteen-inch intervals and training them against a 45-degree diagonal trellis. Edward VII, who ate the best of what the Victorian world offered, said his favorite dish was a single pear, perfectly ripened and perfectly poached.

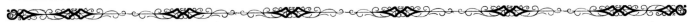

**BELOW:** *Ornamental grasses are still fashionable.* **BELOW, RIGHT:** *The cover of Owen Jones'* The Grammar of Ornament *puts his design principles into practice.* **OPPOSITE PAGE:** *The ottoman was often used in public buildings, such as art galleries and railroad stations. Sometimes, though, it was placed in large central hallways of private homes. The center was often embellished with a plant-filled urn.*

## ORNAMENTAL PAPER WORK

Many Victorians decorated their homes for special occasions with artificial flowers and other decorative items made out of tissue paper, crepe paper, silk, and velvet that they made themselves, a practice that remains popular to this day. Froebel, the late Victorian German innovator in the education of children, made paper folding and paper cutting one of his sixteen "occupations" for children.

© Nance S. Trueworthy

## ORNAMENT BOOKS

Victoriana lovers whose exposure to Victorian ornament has taken place in well-regulated doses are usually ill-prepared for the visually intoxicating deluge of pattern and color contained in Victorian ornament books. After soaking up one or more of these books at a single sitting, later observers might be more understanding and forgiving of Victorian interior decoration, which sometimes strikes critical eyes as drunken. It plainly took a cool sensibility to remain sober in the midst of so many attractive and addictive images; the same is required from those who use them today. Some of the most famous, which have recently been reprinted, are *The Grammar of Ornament* (1856), Owen Jones (1809–1874); *Polychromatic Decoration* (1882), George Ashdown Audsley (1838–1925); and *Polychromatic Ornament* (1873), Albert Charles August Racinet (1825–1893).

## ORNAMENTAL GRASSES

The use of everlastings for interior decoration is a late Victorian technique brought back in vogue by the American Country style of decoration, especially in wreath making. Ornamental grasses have also become more fashionable in the landscapes of homes in many different styles other than Victorian. *Vick's Flower and Vegetable Garden* (1878) attributes the late Victorian fashion to the importation of European dyed grasses, even though "this coloring of flowers and grasses is not exactly in good taste." Vick's recommended *Stipa pennata* (feather grass), *Agrostis nebulos*, *Briza maxima*, and *Erianthus ravennae*.

## OTTOMAN SEAT

Early Victorian women got many of their decorating ideas from popular literature. Lord Byron's fashionably naughty *Don Juan* helped make the ottoman seat a typically Victorian piece of furniture. During the regency preceding Victoria's reign, ottoman was synonymous with divan. Also known as a Turkey sofa, for obvious reasons, the ottoman was originally a low, cushioned seat large enough to accommodate several persons that was usually located in a recess. Late Victorians of aesthetic bent made it the essential component of a Turkish cozy corner. Late Victorians of more formal inclination sometimes placed a circular ottoman with an upholstered post in the center (for displaying an imposing potted plant) in the middle of a parlor or ballroom. The ottoman often featured an extravaganza of tufts, buttons, brocaded upholstery fabric, fringe, and tassels.

## OUTDOOR ENTERTAINMENTS

President Theodore Roosevelt was just one of many public proponents of the vigorous outdoor life. Science was discovering the benefits of fresh air and exercise, and the Victorians, who took to all that was new with gusto, were only too willing to try everything. Many outdoor diversions were done, no doubt, because they were inexpensive. In the summer, for example, people went swimming in the neighborhood pond; when it got cold, they ice-skated on the same surface. They also rode bicycles, rowed, played archery, baseball, cricket, lawn tennis, and croquet. (The fashionable lady, of course, had to have a different outfit for each activity.)

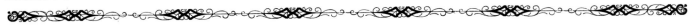

## PAINTED FURNITURE

Early Victorian painted furniture, often called cottage furniture, was made of cheap softwood or an inferior grade of
hardwood. It was commonly painted a light, burnt umber
brown called drab and decorated with painted scrolls
within which appeared vignettes of flowers, seashells,
animals, and landscapes (often with houses in them). This
provided additional employment for early Victorian decorative painters. Late Victorian painted furniture, often called
art furniture, was made of expensive hardwood, often
ebonized to provide a background for artfully designed
patterns of painted ornament, usually of a somewhat
abstracted nature.

## PAISLEY SHAWL

A loom-woven version of the coveted and more costly
Kashmir shawl, the Paisley shawl, which was made in
Scotland, got a real royal boost when none other than
Queen Victoria draped one over her stately shoulders.

## PAPIER MACHE

Basically a laminate of sheets of paper, papier mâché was used by various manufacturers during the Victorian period to create an amazing array of decorative furnishings. It was commonly painted black to readily harmonize with any decor, to provide a neutral background for decoration with paint and wafers of mother-of-pearl, and to imitate the look of old japanned furniture. Some large pieces were attempted, such as chairs and tables, but most papier mâché constructions consisted of small trays, cabinets, fans, and boxes.

## PARIAN/STATUARY PORCELAIN

If a Victorian home didn't have a Staffordshire figure or Rogers group, chances are that it had at least one piece of parian. Parian was first called statuary porcelain because it supposedly imitated ancient Greek Parian marble. It was used to mass-produce both large and small neoclassical decorative items for use in the house or in the garden.

## PARKS

The chief accomplishment of Victorian landscape gardening was the conversion to public parks of Renaissance, Baroque, and Georgian landscapes originally belonging to the aristocracy. Perhaps the most famous Victorian park in Europe was the Bois de Boulogne, more than two thousand acres of forest converted in 1852 to a public pleasure ground with lakes, islands, streams, cascades, rockeries, paths, roads, restaurants, prospects, and the magnificent racecourse called Longchamps. The most famous public park in the United States was Central Park in New York City, designed by Frederick Law Olmsted and Calvert Vaux after they won a competition in 1858. They solved

the problem of crosstown traffic brilliantly with sunken transverse roads and the problems of surface circulation with bridges and separated traffic patterns. Furthermore, Central Park's landscape is a compendium of all that was best in British and French park design. The best European textbook on park design published in the Victorian period is *L'Art des Jardins, Traite General de la Composition des Parcs et Jardins* (Paris, 1879), by Edouard Andre. The best American textbook is *Beautifying Country Homes* (New York, 1870), by Jacob Weidenmann, available today as a reprint.

**OPPOSITE PAGE:** *This combination desk and cupboard features Japonesque motifs on the usual drab background color of Victorian painted furniture.* **ABOVE:** *Since the parlor was the hub around which the wheel of Victorian life spun, it typically was decorated to impress with a combination of overstated furniture, conspicuously displayed art, and collectibles of every possible description; the three parian busts here look like they are right at home.*

🔲 **ABOVE:** *This parlor suite, which consists of a love seat and gentleman's chair, is in the Rococo Revival style. The marble-top center table, which is coffee-table height, is either a reproduction or a cut-down antique; the Victorians did not have coffee tables. The front parlor was the room where guests were received, and, for this reason, was elaborately decorated.* **OPPOSITE PAGE:** *Parquet floors were considered suitable for the entrance hall. In this hallway, the dado is not wood but Lincrusta, which resembles hand-tooled leather.*

## PARLOR FURNISHINGS

As the most public room of any fashionable Victorian home, the parlor was the focus of all its social aspirations and the repository of most of its tangible assets. It was a decorative arts showcase, a miniature museum of art and natural history, a visitor center, and an indoor garden. Despite the strenuous efforts of "art improvers" during the 1870s and 1880s to simplify parlor furnishings and rationalize their design along less vulgar lines, most late Victorian parlors remained cluttered with carpets, pretentiously upholstered furniture, overwrought needlework, objets d'art, and bric-a-brac.

## PARLOR GAMES

The Victorians managed to have an etiquette for every activity, and advice for entertaining guests in the parlor was no exception. By the 1850s and 1860s, whole books brimming with advice were even written on the subject. Although most of these focused on participatory games like charades, tableaux, and versions of musical chairs, twenty questions, and blind man's bluff, there were some that suggested less rigorous and less flirtatious entertainment like reading aloud or spending the long evenings putting together jigsaw puzzles or solving riddles. For an idea of how entertaining these pursuits actually were, leaf through Dickens' *A Christmas Carol* (1843) and see what sport Scrooge's nephew makes of Scrooge when the old miser isn't there.

## PARLOR SUITES

Parlor furniture was sold in sets or suites that consisted of at the minimum a sofa or loveseat, a lady's and a gentleman's armchair, and four armless sidechairs. Larger parlor sets might include a couple of ottomans, a marble-top center table, and six instead of four sidechairs. The extra elements were up to the buyer.

## PARQUET FLOORS

When the Aesthetic Movement scored victories during the 1870s and 1880s in getting late Victorian homeowners to simplify the decoration of their public rooms, such simplification often happened on the floor. Carpets were more of a fire hazard than any other item. It was also argued that carpets were unsanitary, expensive, and difficult to maintain, and that they dominated the decor. By making a concession to pattern in the form of a wood mosaic method called parquet, designers were able to convince progressive late Victorians to reveal the real beauties of their hardwood floors. As long as parquet patterns were flat, all was well. When it was used to create illusions of hills and valleys, however, the results were unfortunate and pretentious. Parquet was either laid by hand or available in prefabricated, canvas-backed sheets.

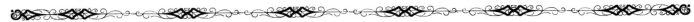

# PATCHWORK QUILTS

While appliqué quilts were usually made for Victorian villas and mansions, patchwork quilts were usually made for Victorian cottages. Based on a mosaic of pieces of fabric cut into geometric shapes, patchwork quilts were made by women of modest means to maximize their fabrics, beautify their beds, and avoid expensive woven coverlets. Appliqué quilts were judged by the inventiveness of the overall design, whereas patchwork quilts were judged by the skill shown in fabric selection, cutting, and the arrangement of the pieces into a standard pattern. Localities did develop subtle variations on standard patterns and gave them charming names, with the result that there are thousands of patchwork designs to choose from today. Most Victorian quilters selected one or two patterns they liked and then spent their lives perfecting their personal style.

# PATENT FURNITURE

The latter part of the nineteenth century could be dubbed the Time of the Three Gs—the gadget, the gizmo, and the gimmick. Nothing reflected this more than patent furniture. This "new and improved" furniture had all of the energy of the Industrial Revolution: it tilted, it revolved, it extended, it folded up, it rocked, it leaned backward, it leaned forward. It served more than one purpose: beds became bureaus, pianos turned into sleeping compartments, tables doubled as washtubs, rockers with attached fans served as primitive air conditioners. Sofas, settees, and lounges changed into everything from beds to billiard tables to bathtubs. Such curious combinations appealed to the imagination of the middle class, who lived in small quarters on even smaller budgets. The patents, issued by the U.S. government for entirely new products or even parts of products like upholstery, braces, or hinges, gave the inventors exclusive rights to the designs.

# PEACOCK FEATHERS

One of the primary symbols of the Aesthetic Movement was the peacock and its feathers. This Oriental motif, which symbolized beauty, showed its colors not only in James McNeill Whistler's famous Peacock Room, but on a host of decorative accessories, from wallpapers to pottery. The Aesthetic Movement never really attracted the attention of the general population, and most people only went so far as to put a couple of peacock feathers into an artistic vase. Not all the famous peacocks in the nineteenth century were artistic renditions; probably to the great distress of his neighbors, the painter Dante Gabriel Rossetti kept live peacocks in his London garden.

# PERENNIAL AND BIENNIAL BORDER PLANTS

"After the bulbs," said *Vick's Flower and Vegetable Garden* (1878), "they give us our earliest spring flowers. Always have plenty of Perennials in a pleasant border, or among the shrubs, and they will supply more flowers, and beautiful ones, for less care and labor than other plants." Vick's recommended adonis, alyssum, aquilegia (columbine), campanula (Canterbury bell), dianthus, delphinium, digitalis, hedysarum (French honeysuckle), hollyhock, honesty (lumaria), ipsmopsis, linum (flax), papaver (hesperis), Brompton stock, sweet William, valeriana, wallflowers, and dictamnus.

**OPPOSITE PAGE:** *When it came to border plants, perennials were recommended.* **ABOVE:** *The wonderful peacock-feather carpeting in this Moorish-style room is new. It was made specially for this Brooklyn brownstone. Peacock feathers were one of the main motifs of the Aesthetic Movement and showed up on everything from fans to painted vases.*

© Nance S. Trueworthy

## PERENNIAL GARDENS

Perennial gardens are better known today as "cottage gardens." A folk gardening tradition based on the use of native and naturalized self-seeding perennials and biennials, gardening with perennials was revived in England late in the Victorian period as an antidote to the excessively formal and fussy carpet bedding and borders of high Victorian villas and mansions decorated in the gardenesque style. Its main proponents were William Robinson, who is more famous for his subtropical and "wild" gardens, and Gertrude Jekyll, who married the Arts and Crafts Movement fondness for vernacular gardening with her personal enthusiasm for the color patterns of French Impressionism. Robinson's ferns and ornamental grasses and Jekyll's cottage gardens are fashionable for all kinds of homes, including Victorian cottages.

## PHOTO STUDIOS

Photography was a newfangled invention that made rapid advances during Victoria's reign. Up until that time, drawings and paintings recorded prestigious places and important people for posterity. Within very little time, however, photo studios sprang up. The studio itself was a spiffed-up version of a family parlor, with the addition of some stiff, uncomfortable-looking props, including some wicker chairs that looked quite outlandish. It took a long time to take pictures; everyone, including the children, was required to sit still for many minutes (no wonder so few of them smiled).

## PHRENOLOGY

Phrenology, the "science" of determining a person's character by examining the bumps on the head, was very appealing to the Victorians. Believe it or not, phrenology enjoyed more than a brief popularity. The head was divided into some thirty-five sections, each of which was assigned a physical or psychological attribute. For example, number twenty, on the forehead, was the repository of wit, while number twenty-five, right above the eye, determined the weight of the person. The doctrine developed by Franz J. Gall in the early 1800s was introduced into the United States by Johann Kaspar Spurzheim, a Viennese doctor, and taken up with a passion by Orson Fowler, the chief proponent of the octagon house. When he wasn't practicing phrenology on the craniums of the rich and famous, Fowler, who had a high forehead, was the publisher of the *American Phrenological Journal and Miscellany*, which, surprisingly, survived well into this century.

## PIANOS AND ORGANS

Victorian women always kept their hands busy. Whenever they weren't sewing or busy at some other handiwork, they were fingering the keyboards of pianos and reed organs. Nothing distinguished a Victorian woman more than her ability to play keyboard music. Enormous quantities of sheet music poured from the lithographic presses of Victorian printers. Every significant event was marked with a song that was published as sheet music, often with an attractive pictorial cover. Much of the music was repetitive and dull, but Victorians were like people today who listen to pop radio—willing to give any new song at least one hearing. The nineteenth century saw the perfection of the pianoforte, which was often housed in an impressive case. Most of the less ornate cases, which housed "cottage pianos," have been destroyed or converted into desks.

**OPPOSITE PAGE, TOP:** *Perennial gardens such as this one, which is spilling over onto the front terrace of this home in Portland, Maine, are also called "cottage gardens."* **BELOW:** *A pipe organ of these dimensions would have lent considerable prestige to a Victorian home; the smaller and simpler reed organ was a far more common instrument.*

© Randy O'Rourke

## PICNICS

To commune with nature and to escape the summer's heat, Victorians planned many types of elaborate outings, one of which was the picnic. Although modern-day picnics are casual affairs with hamburgers and hot dogs, in the nineteenth century, picnics were anything but laid-back. In the quest to enjoy the simple life, the Victorians, dressed in their best, packed up everything but the kitchen sink and transferred it all from the mahogany dining table to the moss table. No proper picnic was complete without several wicker hampers or baskets that held a dazzling array of crystal, china, linens, silver, tea sets, and serving dishes, not to mention all the food, which included everything from an assortment of meats and dainty sandwiches to jellies and fancy cakes.

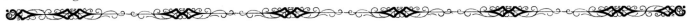

# PICTURE HANGERS

Victorians didn't just put pictures on the walls; they suspended them on cords and wires hooked onto picture rails to give a decorative effect. This practice was popular from the 1870s until about the 1890s, when smaller works of art were often hung by screws hidden in the back. Picture hangers could be plain heavy wire or silk cords from which a tassel hung. Tastemakers had different opinions on picture hangers, but most, like Charles Locke Eastlake, agreed that they should be of colors that blended in with the rest of the decor. "Take care that your picture-cord either matches or harmonises with the colour of the wallpaper behind it," Eastlake wrote in *Hints on Household Taste* (1872). "Sometimes wire, which is almost invisible at a little distance, is used instead of cord. The real advantage of wire is that it does not harbour dust, but it is not so easily adjusted or altered in its length as cord."

© Lincrusta Frieze ® Crown Berger Ltd

🔲 **ABOVE:** *Pictures were hung from silk cords along picture rails, wooden moldings that went around the perimeter of the room. There were several schools of thought, not only on the proper pictures for each room but on the method of hanging. The classical-motif frieze is Lincrusta, which is still sold today.*
**OPPOSITE PAGE:** *Pieces of furniture that are pierced-carved look like lace. In general, pierced carving adds a lot to the value of the piece. This Rococo Revival sofa, with its intricate pattern, is a stunning example.*

# PICTURE HANGING

Before the 1870s, when the wall began to be divided horizontally for decorative treatment, pictures were skyed—placed high up the wall, one above the other, tilting forward at odd angles—so that they reached the ceiling.

"Picture-rings are generally fixed at the back of the frame, and some inches below its upper edge; this throws the picture forward, which some people consider an advantage," Charles Locke Eastlake wrote in *Hints on Household Taste* (1872). This practice, he wrote, "though sometimes desirable in the highest row of a crowded gallery," is not suitable with a picture rail. "Moreover," he continued, "a light frame thus suspended is never steady, but liable to rock with the slightest motion. A better plan is to screw the rings on the upper edge of the frame, which will then lie flat against the wall."

Eastlake and other reformers believed that pictures should be attached to a picture rail and be hung at eye level in a single row around the room.

# PICTURE RAIL

At a time when art was considered essential to the cultivation of taste and to the decoration of a room, the Victorians spent a great deal of time discussing not only which pictures to hang and which should hang next to each other, but how to hang them. The picture rail, a thin wall-mounted strip (usually wood) that went around the room, developed along with the dado-filler-frieze division of walls in the 1870s, and allowed pictures to be hung without harming the plaster or the wallpaper. The picture rail,

which made it easy to rearrange artwork, could be placed next to the ceiling or right under the frieze if the room had one.

## PIERCED CARVING

Cabinetmaker John Henry Belter was the master of the pierced-carving technique, in which portions of the carving of a piece of furniture are cut away or pierced so that the rest of the carving stands out. This lacy look requires great skill to achieve. Belter's pierced-carved pieces are stunningly delicate in appearance because his lamination process accentuates the slender frames of the furniture.

## PIER GLASSES/ OVERMANTEL MIRRORS

Pier glasses were tall, narrow, gilt-framed, French plate-glass mirrors located between a pair of windows and above a marble-topped console table or pier table. Elegant parlors of the early Victorian period featured one or two pier glasses, depending on the size of the room. Like any large mirror, pier glasses magnified the apparent size of the room, reflected light, and monumentalized any precious object placed on the pier table in front of it. The same effects in interior decoration were achieved by overmantel mirrors, the most famous of which was the one Alice went through in *Through the Looking Glass and What Alice Found There*, by Lewis Carroll.

© David Phelps

**ABOVE:** *The overmantel mirror is the focal point of this late-nineteenth-century interior. When lighted, a candelabra on the mantel would have made the mirror's gilded frame glitter even more brightly.* **OPPOSITE PAGE:** *The elegant design of this outdoor plant stand has classical roots.*

## PILLOW SCARVES

The most elegant Victorian linen sets for beds had pillow scarves—richly embroidered and elaborately finished rectangles of cloth placed as dust covers over the pillows. Victorian scarves currently identified as piano, desk, or cabinet scarves may in fact be pillow scarves. Some of the most expensive linen sets sold today once again feature pillow scarves.

## PLANT STANDS

Bent-wire plant stands were designed as portable racks for the interior and exterior display of potted plants. Plant stands made of wood and lined with metal were often built inside bay windows. Freestanding plant stands made of metal, pottery, bamboo, or rustically arranged wood branches, sometimes called jardinieres, were used inside and outside for the display of specimen plants. Fancy Victorian wire plant stands are still being made.

## POCKET DOORS

Pairs of wood-paneled doors that slid into special pockets hollowed out of the thick walls in Victorian houses were common in parlors. Pocket doors were used to separate the parlor from the entrance hall and to separate the back parlor from the front parlor. They were ideal for staging plays or for other home entertainments because they could be closed between acts. Pocket doors were decorated just like the woodwork in the rest of the room. As styles changed, pocket doors were often pushed into their pockets and covered up, only to be discovered years later under layers of paint and paper.

© Nancy Hill

## PORCELAIN

Making porcelain—a thin-bodied ceramic capable of transmitting light—was the goal of European ceramics ever since Marco Polo brought back from China what he called *porcellana*. It was always an elite ware, and it was a conspicuous feature of interior decoration in Victorian villas and mansions. It was generally recognized, despite valiant efforts by English porcelain makers, that the best porcelain was Continental, especially French. The most popular Victorian porcelain in the United States was Haviland-Limoges, the clever product of a New York ceramics dealer named David Haviland. Beginning in 1839, he tried various methods to get potteries in Limoges to make English shapes and painted decorations in French porcelain for the American market. In 1846 Haviland established its own factory in Limoges to do just that. Haviland-Limoges quickly became fashionable porcelain in the United States during the Victorian era.

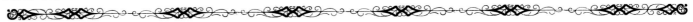

## PORTE COCHERES

The most elegant accommodation for the arrival and departure of Victorian carriages was the porte cochere, a porch with wide openings at ground level extended forward from the front entrance or a special carriage porch leading to a carriage entrance on the side of private and public Victorian buildings. This practical as well as ornamental feature provided protection from the elements for "the carriage trade" during entry and exit.

## PORTIERES

Late Victorian interior designers were able to do away with doors and begin the open planning that would characterize modern interiors of the twentieth century by a device called a portiere. It was a drape, often made with bands of rich textiles hung from a brass or wooden rod, and positioned in line with the dado-foil-frieze demarcations of the walls. Whenever an opening was required, the portiere was tied back or pulled back over a large, decorative tieback. At other times it appeared to be an extension of the wall.

## POSEY HOLDERS

Also called tussie mussies, posey holders are portable bud vases and are as rare and beautiful as lady's slippers in full bloom. Every respectable Victorian woman was expected to have at least two or three for various occasions. The tussie, or knot of flowers, preferably from that someone special, was placed atop the cone-shaped funnel of filigree and was kept fresh by a mussie, or piece of moistened moss. Some of the smaller ones were worn as bodice brooch bouquets to ballroom dances; others had delicate chains attached to rings so they could be added to chatelaines or worn on the finger. Still others had stalklike tripod legs so they could be set atop a dinner table.

## POTTERY

While porcelain was used for Victorian villa and mansion entertaining, pottery—heavy, opaque earthenware— was used for cottage entertaining and functionally in all kitchens. The most popular kind of "cottage china" in the United States during the Victorian era was Tea Leaf Ironstone, a white ironstone imported from Staffordshire that featured tea leaf decorations in copper luster.

## POTTIER & STYMUS

The New York City furniture company Pottier & Stymus, established in 1859 by cabinetmaker Auguste Pottier (1823–1896) and upholsterer William Stymus, was noted for its mastery of the Renaissance Revival style. At the Centennial in 1876, Pottier & Stymus received a commendation for its work.

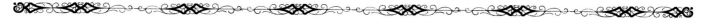

🔲 **OPPOSITE PAGE:** *This colorful portiere divides the dining room from the parlor in this home without abruptly truncating the living space.* **RIGHT:** *This Renaissance Revival side chair by Pottier & Stymus showcases the exquisite craftsmanship of the New York firm in its woodworking and gilt incising.* **BELOW:** *Pressed glass, which was less costly than cut-and-engraved glass, came in a variety of patterns.*

## PRESIDENTIAL CHINA

There is no better index of fashionable taste in ceramics in Victorian America than the sets of state china purchased during various presidencies. Haviland-Limoges, an American firm manufacturing porcelains in Limoges, France, was an acceptable compromise between patriotism and taste, so no presidential china was made in the United States.

## PRESSED GLASS

Like kerosene lighting, which was the people's light and thus rarely seen in fashionable settings, pressed glass was the people's glassware. The process of its manufacture is entirely a nineteenth-century development and is still used today for cheap glassware. Much of it was colorful; some of it was handsome, if not beautiful; and all of it is collectible, usually on the basis of patterns. The process was almost exclusively used for making tableware, decorative vessels, and other bric-a-brac for modest homes, but it was also used in 1840 to make small windowpanes in a Gothic Revival pattern.

## PRANG, LOUIS

Although Louis Prang (1824–1909) is noted for perfecting chromolithography in the United States, he is best remembered for popularizing the Christmas card. In 1880, he sponsored a competition for the best card.

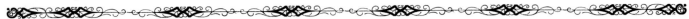

# PRISONS AND JAILS

To Victorian-age thinking—which exhibited an enthusiastic belief in the perfectability of humanity—prisons and jails, like hospitals and asylums, were necessary not only as civic institutions, but as monuments to human fallibility. Despite efforts of reformers to humanize Victorian prisons and jails, however, these buildings were grim and gruesome places because Victorians also believed that architectural environments were capable of altering deviant behaviors. Prisons in the United States often headed the list of attractions distinguished visitors like Alexis de Tocqueville and Charles Dickens wanted to see. The most prominent architect of prisons was British émigré John Haviland, whose surviving (but unoccupied) Eastern State Penitentiary (1823–1829) in Philadelphia is described in Dickens' *American Notes*. During the twentieth century, as institutionalized human frailty is taken out of the city and hidden in the remote countryside, the adaptive reuse of these impressive examples of urban architecture presents one of today's most difficult preservation problems.

# PUDDLING

Until the last quarter of the nineteenth century, when reformers literally straightened out curtains, it was recommended that the finished length of a drape be a couple of feet longer than the distance to the floor so the fabric would fall in folds and puddle to the ground. This puddling was necessary to make the length look right during the day, when the drapes were tied back.

# PUGIN, A.W.N.

Long before anyone else really thought about it, Augustus Welby Northmore Pugin (1812–1852) suggested—as early as the 1830s—that England embrace the Gothic Revival style. By the time he was commissioned to redecorate the Houses of Parliament in 1844, Pugin was the nation's expert on the style. He designed thousands of medieval-style furnishings for the House of Commons and House of Lords and produced nine major books before dying at the age of forty after a brief period of insanity.

# PUTTI

Usually seen cavorting on the C- and S-curves of Rococo Revival furniture, *putti* are cherubs and cupids. The singular of this Italian word is *putto*.

**ABOVE:** *This Renaissance Revival armchair, with its gilded putti lounging on the crest and arms, is by Pottier & Stymus.* **OPPOSITE PAGE:** *The lace curtains in this room, even though they are held by a tieback, still puddle luxuriously to the floor. This is a modern use of the technique; the Victorians would have had the outer draperies puddle, too.*

## QUOINS

The most impressive way the corners of Victorian neo-classical buildings were distinguished was with quoins, rectangular blocks of ashlar or its imitation in wood, plaster, cast-iron, brick, or sheet metal, which were often dressed in ornamental fashion. A practical benefit of quoins was that they could be combined with wall surfaces of materials other than stone, such as clapboard, flush-boarding, brick, or stucco.

## QUEEN ANNE ARCHITECTURE

"Queen Anne," the most popular variety of late Victorian domestic architecture, was also the most inaccurately named, for its references to versions of European vernacular or folk buildings of the late Middle Ages had little to do with the early-eighteenth-century neoclassicism of Britain's Queen Anne. The Queen Anne style was a delightfully adolescent and fussy romanticism of "Mansions of the Olden Time." This vague and generic, but useful, term was compromised in the 1950s by a Yale University architectural historian named Vincent Scully, who invented the terms "Stick Style" and "Shingle Style" to categorize Queen Anne architecture in an effort to link late Victorian domestic architecture to modern domestic architecture of the twentieth century. The result has been to reserve the term "Queen Anne" for a late Victorian house with ornamentally textured surfaces (but without decorative flat-boarded patterns or shingle skins) that doesn't look like any other "name brand" Victorian style. The patternbook house designs of Palliser and Palliser in the 1880s and George Francis Barber in the 1890s, especially those with highly picturesque rooflines, eccentric surface patterns, and a turret or two, are generally called Queen Anne.

© John Kosmer

**ABOVE:** *If it's a late Victorian house and it doesn't fit into any other architectural category, it is usually Queen Anne. Queen Anne homes are often noted for their verandas and rounded towers.* **OPPOSITE PAGE:** *The quoin is one of the most elegant characteristics of the Victorian building; it lends textural variation and visual rhythm to the rectilinear building form.*

© Terry Wild Studio

## RAILINGS AND PARAPETS

Two of the biggest casualties of neglect are porch and veranda railings, which were made in a variety of patterns using turned balusters, sawn-out boards, machined ornaments, and assembled sticks. Even bigger casualties are the parapets of early and high Victorian porches, balconies, and gables. Millworks now supply reproduction railings for the restoration of Victorian porches and verandas, but there has not been a corresponding demand for Victorian parapets, even though they are often necessary to bring the exterior decoration of many Victorian buildings to their original and logical conclusion.

## RAILROAD STATIONS

Having a railway line was a life-or-death situation for most Victorian villages and towns, and the railroad station—often designed by a famous architect like H.H. Richardson—was therefore an object of survival as well as civic pride. Many still stand along today's suburban commuter lines, although few continue to function as passenger stations, having been converted into homes, shops, or restaurants. The city railroad station has been the focus of dramatic preservation battles both won and lost. Many stations have been saved more for the value of their interior retail space than for their beauty, even though their exteriors functioned as the symbolic gateway to the city.

## RENAISSANCE REVIVAL FURNITURE

Just as early Victorian Grecian neoclassical architecture was modified in the 1850s and 1860s to become Italianate and Mansardic, so too out of the early Victorian neoclassical furniture there emerged at the same time a French neoclassical furniture now called Renaissance Revival. Peppered with architectural elements and Renaissance motifs, it was characterized by rich veneers, marble tops, marquetry panels, and plenty of upholstery.

## ROCK GARDENS

"Avoid spotting your lawn," warned Frank J. Scott in *Art of Beautifying Suburban Home Grounds* (1870), "with those lilliputian caricatures on Nature and Art called rock-work." William Robinson, in *Parks, Promenades, and Gardens of Paris* (1869), ridiculed the plastered-over pile of rocks in Edouard Andre's Parc des Butes Chaumont. Andre, in turn, was highly critical of rock work in his *L'Art des Jardins* (1879). Evidently, it was something many people

with means felt compelled to do, but something that rarely satisfied its critics—from which anyone in the late twentieth century tempted to make a rock garden should extract the warning that it is an extremely difficult landscaping technique to master.

## ROCKING CHAIRS

It is pointless to argue about who invented the rocking chair, since it was a folk seat known in many places, but it was especially associated with Victorian cottages in the United States. It was made in different materials, including bentwood, bamboo, twigs, wicker, and rattan. A form of rocker in a Windsor style, called a Boston rocker, was made and named as such throughout the nineteenth century. It was ordinarily painted black and often featured decorative painting on the cresting of the back. Shaker rockers were also made throughout the nineteenth century.

## ROCOCO REVIVAL FURNITURE

French neoclassical styles, including Renaissance, Baroque, and Rococo, were potent forces in Victorian decorative arts from the 1840s to 1870. Rococo Revival, with its curvilinear forms and ornate carving, appeared in such famous Victorian furniture as that produced by Belter and Thonet, but its greatest impact was felt on upholstery fabrics, window treatments, and wall decorations. Rococo motifs were easy work for jacquard weaving machines and the diemakers who made molds for stamping out thin brass rocaille for high Victorian valances. Decorative plasterers were also

adept at making rococo panels on walls, which were subsequently filled with paint, wallpaper, textiles, or decorative painting.

© Kent Oppenheimer

**OPPOSITE PAGE:** *Railings took a variety of intricate forms and were made of many materials.* **LEFT:** *Rocking chairs were found in cottages and middle-class private rooms, such as bedrooms. In the beginning, invalids or elderly people were the main users. As time passed, the mechanics improved, and rockers found a larger following, but were never acceptable in the front parlor. Most rockers were made in simple styles.* **ABOVE:** *Rococo Revival furniture had its heyday in the 1860s. After the Civil War, the North advanced to other styles, but the impoverished and war-weary South kept the old-fashioned pieces. These Rococo Revival chairs are grouped around a table that has a Rogers group statue in the center.*

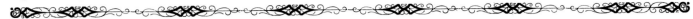

© Richard Sexton

## ROGERS GROUPS

After the Civil War, many American middle-class parlors boasted at least one Rogers group—a sentimental statuette cast in plaster and painted in a light burnt umber called drab that illustrated genre events or scenes from famous plays and poems. Like many successful popular artists, John Rogers (1829–1904) would have preferred to have been known for fine art. His gift, however, was not for the monumental and heroic sculptures of neoclassical idealism promoted by elitist Victorian art critics, but for the genial realism admired by common people. He, more than any other person, was responsible for putting sculptural art in late Victorian homes from coast to coast. The best collection is at The New York Historical Society.

## ROLLER SHADES

Victorian villas, as well as cottages, used fabric roller shades inside their windows to control solar heat gain, ultraviolet deterioration, and radiant heat loss. Roller shades were available in a wide range of colors. It was fashionable during the early Victorian period to ornament them with decorative painting of baroque and rococo scrolls, landscapes, and floral arrangements, which were visible only when the shade was in use. Late Victorian roller shades were available in the tertiary hues fashionable at the time and were decorated with gilded and contrasting color dadoes at the bottom, which were visible at all times. A tasseled pull was another decorative detail that was always visible.

## ROLLING PINS

Glass rolling pins with an open end for receiving ice water to facilitate pastry-making originated as functional devices, but they eventually were decorated by various means to qualify as sentimental gifts. Yet even in the strictly functional wooden rolling pins, there was such delightful variety in materials and profiling that today's Victoriana lovers often adorn their kitchens with them.

## ROMANESQUE REVIVAL ARCHITECTURE

During the nineteenth century, the only revival style dominated by a single architect was the Romanesque Revival of Henry Hobson Richardson (1838–1886), hence it is popularly known as Richardsonian Romanesque. The energized stone masonry of his railroad stations, libraries, churches, and commercial buildings was famous in his own time and was remembered long after his premature death (largely due to overeating) at the age of forty-eight.

## ROOF ORNAMENTS

Victorian Revival designs of the late twentieth century are usually weakest in their ornamentation of rooflines with finials, ridges, edgings, and crestings. Patterns for such ornaments exist in Victorian architectural patternbooks or building material catalogs (some present-day architectural metalwork manufacturers continue to make Victorian roof ornaments), but these structural features tend not to be put on Victorian Revival buildings or put back on original Victorian buildings. Many people seem to have forgotten that one of the most highly desired features of Victorian buildings was their picturesque skylines—especially those edged with filigree to blend the rooflines into the sky.

## ROOFS

Victorian architects utilized roofs as potent architectural elements, something that Victorian Revival designs in the late twentieth century generally fail to recognize. Victorian architecture was more than a simple catalog of roof shapes, of course, but certain popular styles, like the Mansardic, were identifiable primarily by their double-pitched roofs. As the following quotation from Andrew Jackson Downing's *Cottage Residences* (1842) reveals, architectural messages were conveyed by roof pitch, gable exposure, and eave projection. "A Swiss chalet, with its drooping, shadowy eaves, or an old English cottage, with its quaint peaked gables, each embodies a sentiment in its peculiar form which takes hold of the mind, and convinces us that it has living power."

© Nancy Hill

**OPPOSITE PAGE:** *During the last century, roller shades were often painted with scenery and were considered part of the window's decoration. Here, modern versions are used under lace curtains.*
**ABOVE:** *In the Victorians' hands, roofs weren't merely the tops of houses; they were fashionable "top hats," design elements made of various materials.*

# ROSE BEDS

"There are no worse misplantings in most old grounds," fumed Frank J. Scott in *Art of Beautifying Suburban Home Grounds* (1870), "than old rose-bushes, whose annual sprouts play hide-and-seek with the rank grass they shelter. Their bloom and foliage is always finer in cultivated than in grassy ground. Mass them where they can be cultivated and enriched together." One of his examples looks like a six-toothed gear in plan with fourteen varieties arranged in three circles, "where the distance of each circle from the centre may measure the distance from one plant to another in that circle." Around the center post are Baltimore Belle (blush white) and Queen of the Prairies (light red) for June bloom, Mrs. Elliott (purple) and Pierre de St. Cyr (pale rose) for autumn flowers. "In the circle three feet from the center are places for six hybrid perpetual or Bourbon roses of strong growth; and on the outside, six smaller and bushy varieties of the Noisette, Tea, or China varieties in three sorts, so that each little mass or projection of the bed will form a group of low rose-bushes with flowers of contrasting colors."

# ROSES

During the nineteenth century this genus was called the Queen of Flowers, and most authors commented on the astonishing variety of species. Frank J. Scott, following the lead of many nurserymen in *Art of Beautifying Suburban Home Grounds* (1870), simplified the confusing mass of species by arranging them in two divisions: "all roses which bloom in June, and not afterwards; all which bloom more than once in a season." In the division of hardy June roses Scott listed six classes: Hybrid China; Hybrid Provence, Damask, and French; Moss; Climbing, especially hardy Prairie Boursault and Ayrshire and Tender Multiflora and Evergreen; Yellow Austrian; and Wild Bush. In the division of hybrid perpetual roses Scott listed four classes: Perpetual Moss; Hybrid Perpetuals, especially "the magnificent newer *General Jacqueminot*"; Bourbon; and Noisette, Tea, and China. There has been a significant effort in the late twentieth century to make old rose species commercially available, especially those that retain their fragrance after being picked.

# ROSEWOOD

Rosewood, a finely grained, expensive wood from Brazil, was used in making some of the best furniture of the Victorian era. It has a reddish cast and gives off the faint scent of roses when it is being cut, hence its poetic name.

# ROUX, ALEXANDER

Frenchman Alexander Roux came to New York City to set up his furniture shop in the 1850s and worked mainly in the Rococo Revival and Renaissance Revival styles. Under the management of his son, the company continued to flourish nearly until the turn of the century.

© Derek Fell

# ROW HOUSES

After the Great Fire of seventeenth-century London and the subsequent rebuilding, which provided the prototype for the famous eighteenth-century Philadelphia row house, the majority of urban housing consisted of masonry structures. Rural romanticism, however, thrives in the late twentieth century as if Andrew Jackson Downing, who despised Victorian cities and their brick row houses, had never died. This romanticism has resulted in an unbalanced advocacy of rural and suburban Victorian homes relative to the far more numerous, yet equally interesting, row houses most Victorian patternbooks called city houses.

**OPPOSITE PAGE:** *The rose, the most romantic of flowers, is the one bloom most associated with the Victorian era. According to "the language of flowers," a red rose symbolizes love, a yellow one means jealousy, and a white one signals that "my heart is always free."* **ABOVE:** *San Francisco is famous for its candy-colored row houses.*

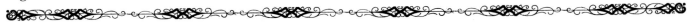

## RUGS

Although large carpets were fashionable during most of the nineteenth century, small rugs always had a part to play on the floors of lesser rooms, especially bedrooms, where they enlivened the straw matting, canvas, or drugget often used to cover the floor. Oriental rugs, often called Turkey carpets, were used during the late Victorian period on small tables in imitation of the Dutch seventeenth-century manner. Rugs came into their own as fashionable floor coverings only in those progressive late Victorian interiors where parquet floors had replaced wall-to-wall carpets. In that context, they were used to direct traffic through the open planning also characteristic of those interiors and to create spatial zones in front of the fireplace, inglenook, bookcase, etc. The old-fashioned hooked rug was revived as part of the Colonial Revival romanticism of the 1890s.

## RUSTIC FURNITURE

From 1840 to 1870, the Victorians made a conscious effort to get closer to nature, devising what has come to be called the Rustic Style. By using branches, moss, twigs, and even bark and roots of plants, both city dwellers and their country cousins created quirky furnishings that were originally intended for the summerhouse and the garden. Although the threat of insect infestations kept most rustic furniture out of the parlor, as time went on, the style found a small niche inside the house.

Women were encouraged to add the skill of making rustic picture frames to their repertoire, and Catherine E. Beecher and Harriet Beecher Stowe, in *American Woman's Home* (1869), recommended making rustic frames out of twigs as a way to save money, and gave detailed instructions for their construction. Other frugal people recommended making frames of waxed and pressed leaves.

If anything, the Rustic Style was participatory in nature; half of the excitement was walking through the woods to find the right materials. *American Woman's Home*, for example, suggests that children make Rustic Style hanging plant baskets out of cheap wooden bowls they have covered with different-colored twigs and sprays of trees. (In cases where no natural materials were at hand, the Victorians used their ingenuity and even came up with needlework projects like the moss mat, a crocheted, mossy-looking substance made out of green and brown wools that was sheared and singed to give it an authentic outdoors look—just so they could put it under the lamp on the center table.)

London's Crystal Palace Exhibition of 1851 and Philadelphia's Centennial of 1876 gave big boosts to the style, and it soon branched out, with cast-iron garden benches, painted landscapes, and even the title pages of books and other paper products echoing the theme.

## SCENT BOTTLES

Although Victorian women were wont to be wary of heady perfumes, they did indulge themselves with some sweet, innocent-smelling scents, which they kept in beautiful cut-glass scent bottles on their dressers. In the great Age of Swooning, when wasp-waisted women could scarce take a breath, much less a step without fainting in the most fashionable manner, smaller scent bottles filled with smelling salts were carried about in beaded handbags. The double scent bottle, a cylindrical vessel of colored cut glass that paired the perfume bottle with the smelling salts container, was a Victorian innovation that made its appearance in the 1850s. Although double scent bottles were made in metal and porcelain, they are rare.

## SCREENS

Among the menagerie of useless things that decorated Victorian parlors and drawings rooms, screens stood out as some of the few practical items. Screens kept sun off the carpet, blocked drafts, shaded eyes from bright light, obscured openings without doors, concealed infrequently used doors, divided large rooms into more intimate areas, segregated areas for children, hid essential but ugly appli-

**OPPOSITE PAGE:** *Area rugs, especially Turkey carpets, became popular in the latter part of the Victorian era.* **ABOVE:** *Perfumes and colognes were kept in pretty scent bottles that also served as dresser decorations. Fragrances that smelled like roses or violets were considered innocent enough for women to wear.*

**ABOVE:** *Decorative screens were used in several rooms of the house as informal room dividers. Mark Twain, for instance, had a screen in the dining room of his Hartford, Connecticut, house, behind which his servant stood between courses of meals. This screen is decorated with hundreds of pieces of Victorian scrap.* **OPPOSITE PAGE:** *The Victorians were avid gardeners and ordered their seeds from catalogs.*

ances such as the refrigerator, and provided an emergency area, often for the resuscitation of women who had fainted. They were made from anything stiff, including wood, bamboo, brass, and papier mâché. Anything colorful, flat, and capable of being worked into a pattern was used to decorate the panels, including embroidery, leaves, pressed flowers, grasses, textiles, printed pictures, paintings, and watercolors. They were used throughout the nineteenth century, but appeared in the greatest variety during the late Victorian decades. Most of the latter examples were decorated at home by aspiring Aesthetic Movement "art amateurs."

## SEED CATALOGS

One of the Victorian traditions of horticultural decoration that survives in the late twentieth century is the winter arrival of spring seed catalogs. Victorian seed catalogs are interesting collections of gaudy color covers, charming illustrations, and nostalgic texts. They are more valuable today as primary documents about Victorian planting practices, necessary for anyone wanting to re-create a Victorian garden or landscape specific to a time and place.

## SERVANTS

Victorian children were allowed to be seen during social events as long as they were rarely heard. The rule for servants was more strict: they were never to be heard and rarely to be seen, but were nevertheless the persons who made the functioning of a sociable Victorian home possible. During grand occasions servants would have been appropriately dressed and much in evidence, but at all times they were in harmony with the decor. During the Victorian period, when servants were plentiful and inexpensive to

hire, the complexity of interior decoration, clothing, cookery, and entertaining increased to employ them. When the availability of cheap land in the American West, in Australia, and elsewhere in the British Commonwealth began to sap the servant class in the late nineteenth century, simplicity in all those departments increasingly became a necessity as well as the fashion.

## SEWING BIRDS

Even when an item was strictly utilitarian, the Victorians found a way to make it decorative, too. The sewing bird is a good example. This metal device, which clamped to the work table and held a piece of fabric while it was being sewn, was shaped like a little bird. Some were fancier than others, but they are all charming, just the same.

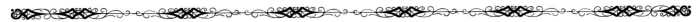
# SHADE TREES

Reading popular Victorian poetry like Longfellow's famous poem about the village smithy working under the spreading chestnut feeds nostalgia for the North American trees of Victorian villages, towns, and roadsides. Despite the realities of disease and a poisoned environment that has decimated the American elm, a spirited effort is under way to reinstate the elm and chestnut as disease-resistant shade trees and to protect the oak, maple, and other favorite varieties.

# SHAKER FURNITURE

Shaker furniture is a pure and simple example of the enduring quality of many Victorian designs. Because it doesn't look ornate and because it doesn't look like anything else Victorian, most people don't associate it with the period, but it was, indeed, made during Victoria's reign. Although the members of the United Society of Believers in Christ's Second Appearing, or Shakers as they have come to be called, originally made the furniture and accessories for their own use, they did begin to cater to the tourist trade as their celibate sect slowly died out. Today, Shaker furniture commands high prices, but reasonably priced reproductions are being made.

# SHAVING MUGS

In the days of the straight razor, when shaving was really a hair-raising experience, every respectable gentleman of means kept his own personalized shaving mug at the local barbershop. (Actually, this wasn't all vanity; individual mugs stopped the spread of the skin disease called barber's itch.) A handled brush, which was swirled around a

cake of soap to create lather, was in each cup. Some mugs merely displayed the gentleman's monogram; others included the name of the owner and a picture depicting his profession. Mugs that depict uncommon professions, such as that of undertaker, are the most sought after today by collectors.

# SHELF CLOCKS

If the domain of the mantel clock was the parlor of Victorian villas and mansions, the domain of the shelf clock was the Victorian cottage kitchen or multipurpose "living room." They were so-called because they sat on shelves, not surprisingly called "clock shelves," especially made for them. Yankee ingenuity, in the form of mass-produced, brass-works, fancy-cased-and-faced shelf clocks, made the old tall-case clock obsolete. Today, some of the most sought-after shelf clocks are calendar clocks.

© Nancy Hill

## SHINGLE STYLE ARCHITECTURE

"Shingle Style" is a stylistic term invented by Vincent Scully in the 1950s to describe the innovative kind of late Victorian American house, derived by H.H. Richardson from the Gothic Revival houses designed by Richard Norman Shaw in Britain and from the Gothic Revival writings of French architect Eugène-Emmanuel Violet-le-Duc, that preceded the modern development of interior space by Frank Lloyd Wright and others in the early twentieth century. Most of the houses cited by Scully as exemplars of the Shingle Style were designed for New England seaside sites where the romantic associations of shingled buildings were most readily connected with the late medieval houses of seventeenth-century Colonial America, which were often shingled and unpainted. Elsewhere, and at the lower common denominator of patternbook Shingle Style, the term is generally used to identify any late Victorian house with an eclectic mixture of medieval-looking forms and a prevalence of shingled surfaces.

## SHOE BUTTON HOOKS

Those high-button shoes that the Victorians were so keen on were not only hard to wear, they were hard to put on. All those tiny buttons had to be buttoned with a shoe button hook. Similar to the glove button hook, it was slightly longer as the buttons on shoes were a trifle larger than those on gloves. Since Bloomingdale's 1886 Illustrated Catalog offered them singly or by the dozen, one would assume that for the well-heeled it was necessary to have a variety. They were about six to ten inches in length and sold for about one to eight cents apiece, depending on the material they were made of. Bone-handled ones, for example, were about five cents each, while more desirable rosewood ones went for six to eight cents each.

⊞ **OPPOSITE PAGE:** *This shelf clock is exactly the sort you might see sitting on a custom-built shelf in the nineteenth century.* **ABOVE:** *This Shingle Style house is painted in the Victorian manner—the details are highlighted in bright colors.*

# SHOPFRONTS

Unlike the upper stories and entablatures of Victorian commercial buildings, which often survive intact within old business districts, most shopfronts have been destroyed in the course of twentieth-century modernizations. Victorian photographs and illustrations reveal their lost architectural delights, along with their glorious signage.

**ABOVE:** *The Victorian shopfront, such as this one in Cape May, New Jersey (a popular resort area in both the nineteenth and twentieth centuries), was designed to have a warm appeal.* **OPPOSITE PAGE:** *With the advent of electroplating technology, everything on the dinner table, from the flatware to the epergne to the tea service, was silverplated.*

# SHRUBS

Shrubs "are the greatest service in the decoration of grounds and the exteriors of buildings," said *Vick's Flower and Vegetable Garden* (1878). Frank J. Scott's *Art of Beautifying Suburban Home Grounds* (1870) offered the sensible advice that "shrubs which are the most commonly known, and the cheapest, are generally the finest, or at least have the greatest number of desirable qualities." At the head of his list Scott placed the lilac (syringa)—"among shrubs in this country it is like the maple among trees, the most common and the most indispensable." Among Vick's recommendations are amalanchier (shad flower/service bush), berberis (barberry), calycanthus (spice bush), colutea (bladder senna), cornus (dogwood), corylus (purple-leaved filbert), cydonia (Japan quince), cytisus (golden chain/laburnum), daphne, deutzia, diervilla (weigela), euonymus (strawberry/spindle tree), exochorda (pearlbush), forsythia, halesia (snowdrop tree), hibiscus (althea/rose of Sharon/tree hibiscus), hydrangea, hypericum (St. John's wort), kerria (Japan globe flower), ligustrum (common privet), philadelphus (mock orange), prunopsis (Chinese double-flowering plum), spirea (bridal wreath), symphoricarpos (snowberry), and viburnum.

# SIDEBOARD

If the fireplace was the heart of the parlor, the sideboard was the soul of the dining room. A large piece of free-standing or built-in furniture filled with shelves and drawers, the sideboard was used to store dishes and other eating utensils and to display food and various pieces of silverplate. Sideboards were often carved with realistic renditions of trussed-up fowl and other dead animals.

## SILHOUETTES

From the eighteenth century through the 1860s, when photography made them all but obsolete, silhouettes cut out of black paper were options for those who could not afford to have their portraits painted. Silhouette cutters traveled from town to town with their scissors. Some people mounted silhouettes in photo albums or pressed them inside the family Bible; others framed them.

## SILVERPLATE

The discovery of Nevada's Comstock Lode in 1859 and of California's Big Bonanza in 1873 made huge amounts of silver available to the Victorians in the United States. Sterling, however, was still too expensive for the middle class. It was only when the process of electroplating was perfected and put into commercial operation in the 1840s that silverplate became the rage. Because it was a new technology, everybody, even Queen Victoria, wanted to have some. It found its greatest use at the dinner table, where everything from the flatware to the epergne was silvered.

## SINUMBRA LAMP

Similar to the astral lamp, the sinumbra was patented in France in 1820. Although the astral and sinumbra were both fueled by Argand burners, their fuel reservoirs were slightly different. Because its reservoir made it virtually shadowless, it was called the sinumbra, from the Latin *sine umbra* and from the French *sinombre*. Like astrals, sinumbras had beautiful glass shades.

© Nancy Hill

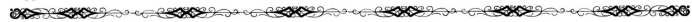

## SLIPPER CHAIR

"Slipper chair," a fanciful appellation for a rather romantic-sounding seat, has recently been proven a misnomer. It seems that the slipper chair was really called a reception chair and was made for show, not for sitting or for putting on dainty silk slippers. It was only in the twentieth century that it went out of style and found itself relegated to the bedroom, where ladies of the genteel persuasion did indeed sit upon it to ease their slippers on and off.

## SMOKE BELLS

Used primarily on hall lighting fixtures, smoke bells were glass or porcelain bell-shaped dishes that were hung over gas and candle-powered fixtures to protect painted ceilings from carbon deposits. They were made in the same styles as the lighting fixtures and were sometimes embellished with etching.

## SMOKING JACKETS

Looser than formal suit jackets and coats, smoking jackets were garments that Victorian men changed into when they wanted to unwind. They were the perfect lounging outfit because they were comfortable, yet with a shirt and tie underneath were considered suitable attire for receiving guests on informal occasions. Popular from the 1850s to the 1890s, they underwent several stylistic transformations before they were replaced in the 1900s by the coat sweater.

## SPATS

"Spats," short for "spatterdashers," referred to the cloth gaiters that Victorian men added to their shoes to keep away the spatters of mud splashed upon them by carriages in bad weather. Ankle-length spats were worn on these occasions, but for sporting events, men opted for nearly knee-length models.

## SPEAKING TRUMPETS

An early version of the bullhorn, the speaking trumpet was used by the captain of a fire brigade to shout orders to his men. Most of the trumpets that survive are presentation pieces, usually of highly decorative silver or silver-plate. During the days of the volunteer bucket brigades, fires usually destroyed everything before they were put out. Today, all types of fire-fighting equipment, including leather buckets, bring enormous prices from collectors.

## SPITTOON

A receptacle into which even the most elegant gentlemen who chewed tobacco spat out the brown juice, the spittoon was a fixture in every house and public building. In the Montgomery & Ward Co. catalog of 1895, a variety of spittoons, or cuspidors, is listed, including a protection cuspidor for twenty-four cents that was secured to a mat twelve inches in diameter, its principal feature being the fact that "it cannot be tipped over." Although most were made of brass, some followed the styles of the day. Some were japanned in red, blue, or green, and at least one made of earthenware sported Gothic Revival arches, crockets, and quatrefoils.

⊞ *The slipper chair started out as a reception chair, which was placed in the entrance hall. It was only when it became unfashionable that it was relegated to the bedroom.*

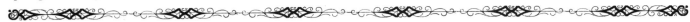

# SPRING CLEANING

If spring cleaning were still done to nineteenth-century specifications, it would take all year to get it done. Every inch of the house, from cellar to attic, was attacked with a vigor unparalleled in history—but not without reason. Moths and other insects were voracious and bothersome intruders that had to be kept at bay. So every surface, from baseboards to the insides of drawers, was dusted, cleaned, and treated with oil of cedar to scare them away. Carpets were taken up, beaten, and stored away if the house was going to be put in summer dress.

Even then the work didn't end; the straw matting for the floor had to be scrubbed, of course. After the woolen blankets were folded up and placed under the feather bed as protection from the winged invaders, the lace curtains still had to be washed and dried, all the upholstered furniture had to be beaten and brushed, and all those dusty statues had to be dipped in starch, which was brushed off when dry. Although some households had servants, most didn't, so all these tasks fell to the housewife and her assemblage of brushes, brooms, and beaters.

# STAFFORDSHIRE FIGURES

The closest most Victorians got to statuary in their homes was a Staffordshire figure or two, usually a pair of sheep, lambs, or dogs. They were enormously popular in early Victorian interiors and were a reliable index of popular taste in the following areas: religion, patriotism, theater, literature, sports, military heroes, and the royal family. Popular prints, including sheet-music covers, were the common source for most figures. Identifying figures is the chief challenge to collectors; known figures are worth considerably more than unknown ones.

# STAIR BUTTONS

An alternative to stair rods, stair buttons were screwed through the carpet to the raise of the stair at the bottom. They came in a variety of decorative designs, and the Montgomery & Ward Co. catalog of 1895 illustrates three that sold for eighteen to fifty cents per dozen.

# STAIRCASES

Many young Victorian women and their families promoted themselves in society by a calculated descent down a well-planned staircase before a capacious hallway filled with potential husbands. Wide landings were not merely the means by which a staircase twisted upward from the first floor; they were stages for dramatic action. The lowest landing was often furnished by the obsolete tall-case clock Victorians romanticized as "the grand-father's clock"; if it struck when a young lady was descending, so much the better. For many Victorian homes, a grand staircase was

© Alan E. McGee/FPG International

the scene of social climbing at its best, and large sums of money were spent on its wood, joinery, surface decoration, and carpeting. Staircase building was always a specialized craft because it required knowledge of geometry and structure as well as joinery. By the end of the Victorian period a great variety of staircase styles was available from specialists like A. Dickey & Co. of Boston, whose *Stairway Design* (1896) illustrated designs in the following styles: Colonial (regular, semicircular, and elliptical), Renaissance, Grecian, Elizabethan, Gothic, and Venetian Composite.

## STAIR RODS

Also called carpet rods, stair rods were brass, iron, or wooden rods used to hold down the stair carpet at the back of the tread; they also served as a decorative element. Many stair rods had pretty finials on each end.

## STEREOSCOPE

Even when it came to recreation, the Victorians liked to be engaged in educational pursuits. The stereoscope, a hand-held wooden viewer that made three-dimensional images, was instructive in history, science, and current events. By inserting a double-image card onto the stereoscope's frame and peering through the lenses, which magnified the picture, the viewer could relive the Civil War and the San Francisco earthquake, travel to London for a visit with the queen, or even gawk at some of the era's brightest stars, for example, Charles Dickens or Mark Twain. From mid-century to the First World War, no parlor was complete without one.

© Dick Dietrich Photography

**OPPOSITE PAGE:** *The central staircase was used in mansions that had mammoth entrance halls.* **ABOVE:** *The stereoscope on the center table was the forerunner of the television set. The Victorians were immensely interested in science and invented a host of items that had scientific and social applications.*

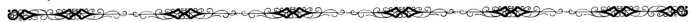

# STICK STYLE ARCHITECTURE

A companion term to "Shingle Style" and likewise invented in the 1950s by Vincent Scully, "Stick Style" describes innovative Victorian wood-frame homes apparently expressing internal structure as external ornament, thus creating the precedent for structural ornament in avant-garde architecture of the early twentieth century. A later generation of architectural historians, more interested in studying Victorian homes in their own terms than as historic precedents of modern architecture, has revealed that the external ornament of many Stick Style buildings does not correlate with the internal structure. Today the term is generally used to identify any late Victorian house with an eclectic mixture of medieval-looking forms upon which sawn-out ornaments and decorative flat-boarding prevail, especially in horizontal bands, vertical rectangles, and X-patterns. Because picturesque Victorian versions of medieval folk buildings in northern Europe, such as the Swiss chalet and the Norman farmhouse, were often polychromed, they were the prototype for the kind of decorative scheme used by American ready-mixed paint companies of the 1870s to promote their new product. The largest concentration of Stick Style homes built after the Civil War was in seaside resort areas.

*© Balthazar Korab*

**ABOVE:** *Stick Style architecture was in vogue during the latter part of the nineteenth century.* **OPPOSITE PAGE:** *Sundials reminded Victorians of olden times, what they liked to call "the good old days."*

# STRAW MATTING

It was customary in the summer to cover the floors with straw, or Indian, matting, but use of the material was not restricted to the floor or the season. In the 1870s, the golden-colored matting was often put on the walls of Aesthetic Movement–style interiors to complement the furniture and blue-and-white china.

At a time when carpeting could be the most expensive element in a decorating scheme, straw matting, which wore out quickly, was seen as a thrifty year-round alternative for some rooms, such as the parlor, that were not much in use. "We have in mind one very attractive parlor which has been, both for summer and winter, the daily sitting-room for the leisure hours of a husband and wife, and a family of children, where a plain straw matting has done service for seven years," wrote Catherine E. Beecher and Harriet Beecher Stowe in *American Woman's Home* (1869).

## SUBURBS

Romanticizing city living and rendering its domestic architecture more picturesque began with John Nash's 1811 plan for Regent's Park in London, which was publicized throughout the world in the splendid illustrations of *Metropolitan Improvements* (1827), by Thomas H. Shepard and James Elmes. The first planned suburb in the United States was New Brighton on Staten Island, New York, designed in 1836 by John Haviland, a British émigré architect based in Philadelphia. The first published model plan for an American suburban village appeared in William H. Ranlett's *The Architect* (1847). Most suburbs were situated near railway and interurban streetcar lines, often on land owned by the transportation companies. The most famous were located near New York City: Llewellyn Park (1853), Garden City (1869), Short Hills (1874), Rochelle Park (1885), and Bronxville (1892). Those near Philadelphia were Chestnut Hill (1854) and the Pennsylvania Railroad's "Main Line" suburbs of the 1860s and 1870s. Roland Park (1891) served Baltimore, and Chicago was served by Lake Forest (1856) and Riverside (1869).

## SUMMER DRESS

When the summer sun began to be unbearably hot, it was time to put the house in summer dress. In the days before electric fans, air conditioners, or even window screens, Victorians who didn't have enough money to go to the country for the duration found other ways to beat the heat. They covered up the floors with straw matting and covered the furniture with cotton or muslin slipcovers. Gauzy mosquito netting was hung over beds to ward off mosquitoes and placed over chandeliers and gilt mirrors to dull the costly shiny surfaces that attracted flies, which left damaging flyspecks. Many historic sites, including New Orleans' Gallier House, continue the custom.

© Nance S. Trueworthy

## SUNDIALS

Long after telling time by sunlight was obsolete, sundials survived as decorative reminders of "the olden time" in the Victorian domesticated landscape. The sundial itself varied little, but its base and horticultural setting were subject to differences in taste. It was most often used as a hub, focal point, or terminus in a pattern of walks or paths.

## SUNFLOWERS

To the artistic proponents of the Aesthetic Movement, the sunflower was much more than a pretty flower or a decorative element that happened to appear on everything from andirons to building facades. It was a symbol of constancy. To the uninitiated, which was almost everyone in the nineteenth century, it became the butt of many jokes about the whole short-lived movement. More than once, its face replaced by none other than Oscar Wilde's, it graced the pages of the English magazine *Punch*. It also got the royal stamp of approval when Queen Victoria suggested it be used on "The Queen's Curtain," a pair of portieres destined for Windsor Castle that were displayed in the British exhibit at the Philadelphia Centennial in 1876.

favorite Victorian subjects. These were considered not only decorative but highly instructive. Many were featured in man-made mini-environments, then placed in glass domes. One of the more interesting treatments was a rare glass-encased fireplace screen filled with all manner of beautiful birds in pursuit of an array of iridescent insects. Sagamore Hill, President Theodore Roosevelt's retreat in Cove Neck, New York, is perhaps the quintessential example of the menagerie principle—its rooms are filled with all sorts of wild beasts.

## TARTANS

The Victorian passion for plaids was in large part due to Prince Albert's decoration of Balmoral, the royal family's Highlands estate. Indeed, so taken with tartans was Albert that he designed one in gray, red, and black that still bears the Balmoral name.

In addition to the Balmoral tartan, to which Victoria was particularly partial, the castle was dominated—some said overpowered—by two other tartans. The scarlet Royal Stuart and the dark green Hunter Stuart were used for carpet and draperies, making the Balmoral estate nearly wall-to-wall tartan. As a tribute to the dear departed Albert, Victoria staunchly refused to change the decor at Balmoral and was forever defending it against critics.

The interest in tartans didn't end with interior decoration. Victoria often dressed her children in kilts when they went to Balmoral, and at one point, ladies even took to putting plaids in their needlework.

## TAXIDERMY

In their never-ending quest to bring nature closer to home, the Victorians took to stuffing both exotic and ordinary species and placing them in the home. Squirrels, pheasants, owls, hummingbirds, and peacocks were some

## TENDER BULBS AND TUBERS

"The Tender or Summer Bulbs are delightful almost everywhere. The Gladiolus takes rank at the very head of the list and the Dahlia is scarcely if any less popular," according to *Vick's Flower and Vegetable Garden* (1878). Edward Sprague Rand disagreed about dahlias in his *Flowers for the Parlor and Garden* (1864): "This once popular flower is fast falling into unpopularity, and will soon be consigned to oblivion. It has seen its best days, and has been compelled to give place to the Gladiolus, Hollyhock, and Double zinnia. It is hard to find what could have given the Dahlia its popularity. It has no grace or growth of flower, is a coarse, rank-growing and smelling plant, and beyond a certain mechanical rosette arrangement of the petal, has nothing to recommend it." Subsequent breeding rescued it from oblivion, but Rand's indictment reveals some Victorian principles of floral beauty. Vick's also listed boussingaultia (Madeira vine), colocasia (*Caladium esculentum*), erythrina, polyanthus (tuberose), tigridia (Mexican tiger flower), and tritoma.

Among the tender bulbs, the gladiolus is one of the most beautiful, coming in a stunning array of colors.

**ABOVE:** *The tête-à-tête was another romantic furniture style. In actuality, it was two chairs linked by a common arm. The chairs often faced opposite directions so the sitters could have intimate conversations without the rest of the world noticing. The tête-à-tête pictured is in the Rococo Revival style. Because it is in front of a pier mirror, the sitters could also cast clandestine glances at each other.* **OPPOSITE PAGE:** *Tiffany's Wisteria Lamp shows his mastery of the medium.*

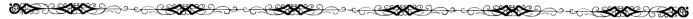

# TETE-A-TETE

The Victorians loved to let this term roll off their tongues. The phrase has a teasing, flirtatious ring. Derived from the French and meaning "a conversation," or literally "head to head," the Victorians used it to describe a very special piece of furniture. The tête-à-tête was a settee scarce bigger than two armchairs where two souls of the opposite gender could commune and perhaps even flirt right under the eyes of society. Often, it took the form of two connected chairs that faced opposite directions, making it more than easy for courting couples to whisper sweet nothings in each other's ears. Its use was not always so romantic; one proud papa hired famed cabinetmaker John Henry Belter to make one for his little twin daughters. There were also all those advertised tête-à-têtes that really were nothing more than plain sofas with fancy names.

# TIEBACKS

Also called curtain bands, tiebacks were decorative devices used to loop or tie back curtains during the day, allowing sun and fresh air into the room. In the evening, the draperies were drawn together for warmth and privacy. Tiebacks could be as simple as silk cords with tassels or as elaborate as stamped gilt depictions of greenery with Bohemian glass flowers. Tiebacks followed the style of the room and carried the appropriate motifs.

# TIFFANY, LOUIS COMFORT

Of all the contributions he made to the field of the decorative arts, Louis Comfort Tiffany (1848–1933) didn't want to be remembered for his lamps. Nevertheless, they are exactly what he is remembered for today. Tiffany, whose father was the founder of Tiffany & Co., was born with not a silver but a gold spoon in his mouth. Louis didn't go into the family firm right away but decided to become a painter, at which he was technically very good, although somewhat uninspired.

In 1879, Tiffany, along with Candace Wheeler, Samuel Colman, and Lockwood de Forest, formed the L.C. Tiffany & Associated Artists interior design firm, which received major commissions from the Seventh Regiment Armory in New York City, Mark Twain in Hartford, Connecticut, and even the White House. The firm disbanded in 1883.

Tiffany's major contribution was made in the field of glass. He made several technical and aesthetic inroads. His first works were church windows. Unlike other ecclesiastical windows of the time, Tiffany's took on a pantheistic theme, with scenes of trees and flowers, not saints. They were quite controversial but eventually were accepted. He continued to experiment with the medium through the years and created exquisite pieces in opalescent and Favrile glass. Unlike his windows, which usually were custom-made, his lamps were readily available and were a big success. One of the most magnificent, the Wisteria Lamp, was actually designed by a female client of his.

Tiffany also designed mosaic-work and metalware, especially candle-holders, desk sets, and jewelry. In each of the fields he worked in, he was considered innovative. When his father died in 1902, he took over as design director of Tiffany & Co.

Although his country house in Oyster Bay, New York, was destroyed by fire, some of Tiffany's gorgeous windows are on permanent display at The Metropolitan Museum of Art in New York City.

## TIN CEILINGS

Developed during the nineteenth century to cover up damaged plaster, tin ceilings were stamped metal panels that imitated costly wood and plasterwork. At the peak of their popularity near the turn of the century, they were also used as wall panels in commercial buildings—stores, offices, restaurants—but not in private homes that had any pretensions to style. They are still being made in a variety of patterns and are still associated with shops. They can be painted with an oil-base paint or coated with polyurethane.

## TOYS

Most Victorians were not wealthy and few had enough money for toys, which would have been considered luxuries. Many parents made toys for their children, and sometimes children made their own, too. When toys were purchased, they usually were miniature versions of household items or machinery—toy stoves, sadirons, steam trains, fire engines, baby carriages, horse carts, scales, dinner bells, toilet sets, and tea sets. By using these toys, children learned their role in life.

Although tops, dolls, wooden soldiers, wooden boats, musical instruments, magnets, blocks, marbles, and banks were popular, it was the mechanical, hot-air, and steam toys that were most attractive. The Montgomery Ward & Co. catalog of 1895 devoted ten of its 624 pages to toys, from the Kicking Mule Bank, in which the animal throws the rider over its head and the coin is thrown from the

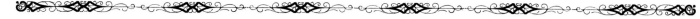

man's mouth into the slot, to the Baby Quieter Wheel Toy, in which a man in a wheeled lounge bounces a baby on his knee when the vehicle moves.

# TRELLIS/PERGOLA/ARBOR

During the twentieth century the Victorian desire for connections between the house and its landscape have been lost. Most of today's surviving Victorian homes look naked and disconnected from their landscapes. Victorian verandas and porches often included lattices behind or between vertical structural members to support flowering climbers like tecoma (trumpet flower) and clematis, of which Victorians were so fond. Prominent blank walls were often enlivened by a decoratively patterned trellis. Victorian homes in neoclassical styles were often connected with their formal, gardenesque landscapes by pergolas. An arbor, often with a garden seat or swing, was a favorite focal feature in the landscape or its boundary.

# TURRETS

Little towers, called turrets, were often the chief ornamental feature of late Victorian buildings. When they had a function, they projected from the upper stories of a building at strategic points for the enjoyment of the prospect. When there was no prospect worth looking at, which frequently was the case in speculative subdivisions, turrets with their "pixie hat" conical roofs provided picturesque rooflines as well as the necessary romantic associations with medieval castles and *châteaux*.

**OPPOSITE PAGE:** *Victorian children amused themselves with a variety of toys, most of which were designed to be educational.* **LEFT:** *Intricate trellises were used to create outdoor rooms. The walls of these rooms were decorated with climbing vines.* **ABOVE:** *This house in Round Lake, New York, sports a tower and a turret.*

🔲 *The upholstery on the furniture in the Victorian era profited from the availability of an increasing variety of colors and comfortable padding, making pieces such as this chair a focal point in the room. The antimacassar and crazy-quilt pillows complete the picture.*

## UPHOLSTERY

Improvements in technology, more than anything else, were the mainspring of the Victorians' changing ideas of upholstery. New types of springs and padding brought comfort; new dyes brought brighter colors and varied shading; looms like the jacquard brought variety; and tufting machines brought more elaborate designs. And for the first time, there was a tremendous selection of fabrics— satin, wool satin, horsehair, moreen, damask, brocatelle, brocade, velveteen, corduroy, plush, chintz, paisley, and plaid—in a variety of colors, including violets, greens, blacks, yellows, blues, reds, and tans.

Indeed, as the century progressed, seating furniture became more padded—and much more comfortable. This culminated in the penchant for Turkish seating furniture, which was all fabric and fringe with nary a stick of wood showing.

Up until recently, historians, curators, and collectors didn't pay much attention to period upholstery. Pieces were routinely stripped of the original upholstery, which did not fare well with the passage of the years, and re-covered in contemporary fabrics. Lately, however, there has been a movement to conserve and copy vintage upholsteries. New techniques of upholstery are even being devised so that the piece of furniture can be reupholstered without damaging the original fabric.

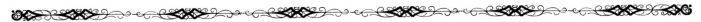

# VASE AND URN GARDENS

Victorian villas and mansions often featured at least one cast-iron urn in the exterior landscape. Many of them escaped twentieth-century wartime scrap drives, yet they often have been left standing empty in the garden—naked but proud. They have been neglected because plant material will not survive in the temperature-sensitive metal's winter daytime thawing and nighttime freezing. The plants must be replanted every spring. Anyone who is capable of planting a window box or hanging basket can

plant a Victorian urn because it accommodates the same plant material and requires the same care. The most popular design concept behind Victorian urn gardens was the fountain, hence urn gardens require a vertical plant in the center, plants that cascade over the sides, and a froth of color between them. Vase gardens were features of the interior landscape. Unlike the outside urn gardens, which obscured the urn when the garden was at its peak, inside vase gardens displayed the decorative features of the vase at all times. Forced bulbs were the most popular plant material for vase gardens.

# VENTILATORS

Ventilators were turrets placed on the ridge or peak of a roof to ornament the louvered or latticed enclosure of the interior ventilation pipes. In *Villas and Cottages* (1857), Calvert Vaux said they "are often useful for convenience and artistic effect. They need to be planned with a proper escape for the water that will find its way into them in

**ABOVE:** *The symmetrical placement of these matching urns gives this prospect a dramatic look.* **OPPOSITE PAGE:** *Of all the features of the Victorian home, it is the veranda that is most attractive. Perhaps the most common domestic Victorian image is of families sitting peacefully on the veranda sipping ice-cold lemonade on a sultry summer day.*

rainy weather." As the late twentieth century has only recently rediscovered, a well-ventilated interior is essential to the health of its inhabitants, so there is a medical as well as aesthetic aspect to their revival. Another kind of ventilator was latticed under porches and verandas, often with clever sawn-out patterns framed within the foundation structure.

## VERANDAS

In *Villas and Cottages* (1857), Calvert Vaux declared that "The *veranda* is perhaps the most specifically American feature of a country house, and nothing can compensate for its absence." That is why so many Victorian verandas have been recently restored, why most Victorian Revival buildings feature verandas, and why a sizable millwork industry has developed to supply the need. Vaux was flag-waving when he associated verandas with American homes. Verandas—sheltered areas with openings parallel to an external wall—were called at various times and places arcades, colonnades, and loggias. The term itself is a seventeenth-century Hindustani word for such areas on Bengalese vernacular cottages, which British residents in India called bungalows. Today, the term is often confused with porch, which is a sheltered area perpendicular to an entrance. Andrew Jackson Downing, who used architectural terminology with more emotion than accuracy, sometimes called a veranda a "piazza," a term that more precisely describes an open area surrounded by buildings, or an "umbrage," from the Italian word for shadow.

© Dick Dietrich Photography

## VICTORIA, THE QUEEN

On the throne for sixty-three years, Queen Victoria (1819–1901) started to rule England when she was only eighteen years old. History has not been kind to her image. Over the years, she has been portrayed as a stodgy, sexually repressed, old-fashioned matron. By all accounts, however, including her personal daily diaries, that is a misconception.

Despite the fact that it was decreed that she should marry, she wasn't really keen on the idea—until she saw Albert, that is. They were married in 1840—she, not he, popped the question—and eventually had nine children, four sons and five daughters. Victoria never really enjoyed her role as a monarch and would have preferred to spend more time with Albert, whom she often described as beautiful.

Despite the fact that she considered Albert the cultured one, she had her own set of accomplishments. She was praised for her singing, and her sketches of her family that have survived are considered more than adequate.

Victoria was devastated when Albert died in 1861, and she continued to mourn for the rest of her long life. One of the effects of her mourning was that she insisted that every-thing be kept as Albert, whom she considered her superior in matters of art and taste, had left it. Between 1861 and 1901, when she died, virtually nothing was disturbed or modernized. When wallpapers and fabrics needed to be replaced, Victoria dutifully ordered copies of the originals.

Victoria gained the respect and affection of her subjects, who all turned out for the Silver Jubilee celebration that marked her half century on the throne. She died, still missing Albert, in 1901, leaving behind an empire upon which the sun never set.

## VILLA STYLE ARCHITECTURE

Most Victorian suburbs in the United States were middle-class "villages in the city," and the villa was the favorite form of domestic architecture for those places, which have largely survived intact because twentieth-century subdivisions still follow the Victorian model. Of the tri-partite Victorian class-conscious paradigm of cottage/villa/mansion, "villa" is the only term in current use, as in "executive villa." Today's villas may not look like Victorian villas, because present romantic fantasies are not those of the Victorian period, but their socioeconomic associations, locations near large cities connected via commuter links, and sitings in landscape gardens would be recogniz-able to any Victorian shown them today. Like so much of early Victorian romanticism, the villa—as well as the suburban landscaped setting—was an early-nineteenth-century Regency creation. The prototypes of Regency vil-las were the Renaissance villas and Tuscan farmhouses of

**BELOW:** *Freestanding houses in the suburbs came to be called villas even though they didn't feature villa-style architecture.*
**OPPOSITE PAGE:** *The wainscoting in this entry hall consists of sections of wallpaper separated by wooden panels. The silver tray on the table is a receptacle for visitors' calling cards.*

northern Italy. Villas had at least two stories, generally appeared to be in some sort of neoclassical style, and sometimes featured a tower, which Andrew Jackson Downing and other Victorian romantics pretentiously, but erroneously, called a "campanile," the Italian word for bell tower.

## VOYSEY, C.F.A.

One of the leading domestic architects of the early twenti-eth century, Charles Francis Annesley Voysey (1857–1941) was also a successful textile and wallpaper designer. His naturalistic patterns had a medieval flavor and often included various birds, vines, and fruits. Some of his wallpapers have recently been reproduced.

Eastlake lamented that "this picturesque old feature of high wainscoting has long been banished, with many others, from modern households" and remarked that, with wainscoting, "the paper was then only required to cover the upper part of the walls, and the effect was far less monotonous than now." It was an expensive treatment, and by the 1880s some companies started offering ready-made wainscoting that was easy to install.

## WAINSCOTING

A type of dado, usually made of wood panels, wainscoting was recommended for halls, entries, and kitchens. Charles Locke Eastlake's *Hints on Household Taste* (1872) popularized it or its imitation for use in all rooms of the house. Although it was usually a three-foot-high band that started at the floor, wainscoting occasionally reached the height of the doorway architraves.

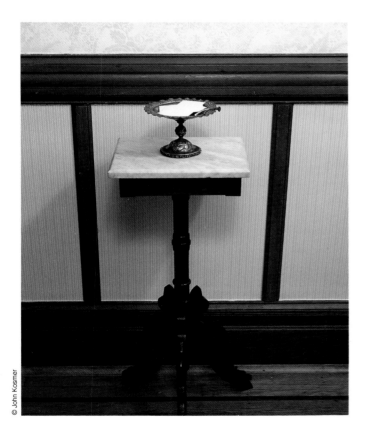

© John Kosmer

## WALLPAPER

The nineteenth century was the Age of Wallpaper. A white wall was indecently dressed, what with the profusion of attractive papers that could be put on it. In the nineteenth century, wallpapers were affordable to the middle class for the first time because of major technological advancements. Many patterns were available because, in addition to the firms in China, England, and France, American manufacturers became well-established, too. Although French papers dominated the market until 1870, American designs were making inroads. As the choice of papers increased, so did the rules for choosing them. By mid-century, there were books that had all kinds of suggestions for styles, colors, and patterns for each room of the house. And between 1870 and 1890, wallpaper became such a dominant decorative element that people were literally papering everything that didn't move, including closets, privies, and ceilings.

With England leading the way with the likes of William Morris, designer wallpaper became all the rage. Walls were divided into three areas—dado, filler, frieze—and each was papered with a different pattern delineated by borders. As the century closed, the dado and its border were eliminated and the frieze became a much wider accent to the paper on the wall.

▨ **ABOVE:** *The Victorian penchant for wallpapers combined with the common tendency to decorate every possible surface often resulted in the wild sort of room treatment seen here, where the ceiling, walls, and carpet have different patterns and color schemes.*

Wallpaper patterns followed and imitated architecture and decorating styles. The century started with lavishly ornate French papers that depicted nature in all its glory; by mid-century the Gothic and Rococo Revival styles dominated. Then the stylized designs of the Aesthetic Movement momentarily took over. But by the 1890s, the French flowers and scrolls were back again.

## WARDIAN CASE

In 1829, Nathaniel Bagshaw Ward of London accidentally invented what is now called the terrarium. After 1851 it was often used to create indoor winter gardens and ferneries in parlors, sometimes on elaborate stands and within glazed panes of glass angled in the shape of an elegant, miniature greenhouse. The English practice was to build the Wardian case into the window casing, sometimes projecting it outside. Edward Sprague Rand's *Flowers for the Parlor and Garden* (1864) suggested extending vitality of winter bouquets "procured from a florist" by putting the stems in wet sand or the earth inside a Wardian case. Although it was a pleasant addition to the interior landscape, Wardian cases played a far more important role in science. They made it possible to protect and transport botanical specimens long distances on ships. Without the Wardian case, the efforts of Victorian plant hunters would have been thwarted.

## WATCH FOB

Gentlemen in the last century carried pocket watches about with them. These watches were attached to fancy decorative chains that were secured to a special pocket just below the waistband of their suits. A series of pretty baubles, called fobs, dangled from the chain, making the whole ensemble quite decorative.

## WATERFRONTS

The commercial success of recent waterfront developments, such as Harborplace in Baltimore and South Street Seaport in New York City, has led to the restoration of previously neglected waterfronts. Unfortunately, the shift from water to land transport, which began with the proliferation of Victorian railroads, has led to the neglect and frequent destruction by shoreline highways of these areas during the twentieth century. None of them exists in its full Victorian glory, and one must survey old pictures or visit Mystic Seaport Museum in Connecticut to get an idea of what they once looked like.

## WAX FRUIT AND FLOWERS

"There are no imitations of natural objects more exact and pleasing than those made of wax," said a guidebook of 1864 published in Boston, "more especially the representations of fruit and flowers. If well made, the most practised eye cannot sometimes detect the real from the artificial." Such artificiality, no doubt innocent enough in its own context, strikes modern observers, even many of those who are devoted to Victoriana, as absurd—a situation not much helped by the faded and bedraggled state of surviving examples. In pristine condition, they were merely part of the flora—alive and dead—decorating early Victorian interiors, and they migrated among the parlor center table, dining table, pier table, and mantel shelf.

# WEDDING CAKES

Weddings typically had three cakes: the wedding cake, the bride's cake, and the groom's cake. The wedding cake, which was the largest, was usually a dark, rich fruitcake with ornate frosting. It was not eaten. After the bride, her handsome groom at her side, cut the wedding cake, it was sealed and stored until their silver wedding anniversary. The other cakes were cut up and boxed for the guests to take home. Sometimes, these cakes were cut beforehand, with the bridesmaids threading narrow strips of them through the bride's wedding ring to give as good-luck favors.

The bride's cake, which was white, and the groom's cake, which was dark, were usually round and decorated in the same way as the wedding cake. They were cut into the same number of pieces as the number in the wedding party. Inside the bride's cake, there were a coin, thimble, ring, and button—items that symbolized the future of the member of the bridal party who got them. The coin meant wealth, the thimble was destined to be the partner for an old maid, and the button was for forlorn sweethearts. The bridesmaid who got the ring, however, was going to be the next bride—and within a year, at that.

# WEDDING GOWNS

Styles of wedding gowns changed along the same lines of everyday fashions, but the Victorian bride didn't always wear white. In most cases, the wedding gown, which would have been quite an expensive purchase, was intended to be worn in succeeding seasons to balls and other formal occasions, with the veil serving as a shawl. Paris gowns by Charles Frederick Worth were the most desirable, but few people could afford them. Most people opted instead for more practical and less expensive versions with veils and trains. Although early in the era most

brides wore virginal white, those women who were living in the wild, wild West, where social occasions were few and far between, usually chose a more practical gown of wool, cambric, or linen from among several colors. By the 1850s, most gowns were white, although some were subtle shades of blue, gray, or plum. By the end of the era, white had established itself as the favorite color.

# WEDDINGS

The word "marriage" referred to the ceremony, and the word "wedding" referred to all the activities that went on before and after the ceremony. After being married at the church or at home, the newlyweds typically hosted a wedding breakfast, which was really a buffet luncheon. (Any reception held before 1:00 P.M. was considered a wedding breakfast.) After the short reception, the couple changed their clothes and went on their honeymoon.

**OPPOSITE PAGE:** *Wedding gowns were not always white, and many brides continued to wear them for the first couple of seasons after their marriage. These lace dresses would have been worn by turn-of-the-century brides.* **ABOVE:** *The wedding cake was an important part of the Victorian ceremony, but it was rarely served by winged* putti.

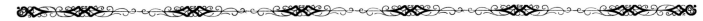

© Gross & Daley

## WHEELER, CANDACE

A partner in Tiffany's Associated Artists, Candace Wheeler (1827–1923) was in charge of textiles and embroidery for the firm. Perhaps the most influential woman in the Aesthetic Movement, she also designed wallpapers, one of which won first place in an international competition in 1881. She wrote several books on interior decoration and was a noted feminist.

## WHISTLER'S PEACOCK ROOM

Considered the preeminent example of an Aesthetic Movement interior, Harmony in Blue and Gold: The Peacock Room is now in the Freer Gallery, which is part of the Smithsonian Institution. The twenty-foot by thirty-two-foot room is the only surviving example of the interior design of painter James Abbott McNeill Whistler (1834–1903). Actually, although the Peacock Room is associated with Whistler, it was Thomas Jeckyll, an architect, who designed it; Whistler painted it.

In 1876, shipping magnate Frederick Leyland hired Jeckyll to decorate the dining room of his new London townhouse. He wanted the room to showcase his impressive collection of Chinese blue-and-white porcelain, antique leather wall hangings, and his Whistler painting *The Princess From the Land of Porcelain*. When the room was nearly finished, Jeckyll consulted Whistler about the color scheme. Whistler wanted to make certain artistic changes and got the approval from patron Leyland, who promptly left town for the summer.

Whistler got a little carried away and painted over every available surface, including all those valuable leather wall hangings. When Leyland came home, he was, to say the least, a bit miffed to find six beautiful gold peacocks strutting proudly across the room. The paintings remained, but the friendship of Leyland and Whistler did not survive.

## WHATNOT

What better place to store all the bric-a-brac and knick-knacks than on the shelves of the whatnot, that parlor fixture that no self-respecting Victorian home was without from about 1850 to 1875? Its graduated open shelves were ideal spots for decorative objects like vases and classical parian busts, as well as for items of a more personal nature like photographic portraits of loved ones and travel and scientific souvenirs like shells and rocks. Because the shelves were open, children found them particularly attractive.

# WICKER FURNITURE

With all its charming curlicues and curvaceous contours, wicker is the undisputed coquette of the Victorian era. Although the Japan craze was carrying Victorians to far-away lands in Asia, wicker was in its golden age. Inexpensive and lightweight, it was a hit with the rising middle class. Initially used on porches, it gradually made its way into the parlor and bedroom as accent pieces to accompany the Japonesque fans and parasols. Later, as its hygienic properties were recognized—its open weave made it a good source of ventilation—it was used everywhere. With the exception of some extremely exotic and overwrought pieces that were used as props in photo studios, wicker furniture was comfortable. Wicker is one of the many contributions of the Victorian era that continued to be popular in the twentieth century.

# WILDE, OSCAR

Ironically, the foremost apostle of the Aesthetic Movement, Oscar Fingal O'Flahertie Wills Wilde (1854–1900), didn't originate any of its ideas. He designed nothing and painted no pictures, but he walked around in his velvet knickerbocker suit with a lily in the lapel and told everyone to love "art for art's sake." Wilde, who once lamented that he couldn't live up to his collection of blue-and-white china, gave the American public a taste of Aestheticism when he went on an eighteen-month tour in 1881 at the same time Gilbert & Sullivan's *Patience*, which satirized Wilde and his friends, opened in New York City.

Wilde was quite a wit and his lectures were highly successful, spawning a whole line of Wilde items, everything from songs like "Oscar Dear" to the Little Lord Fauntleroy suit.

Wilde, who had been an Oxford scholar, often satirized the conventions of Victorian society in his plays and novels. His works include *The Happy Prince and Other Tales* (1888); *The Picture of Dorian Gray* (1891); *Lady Windermere's Fan* (1892); and his masterpiece, *The Importance of Being Earnest* (1895).

At the height of his career, Wilde was accused of having a homosexual relationship, then an offense punishable by imprisonment, and was sentenced to two years hard labor. Three years after his release from prison, his health ruined, Wilde died in France (which was a much more liberal place when it came to liaisons with the same sex).

© Feliciano

**OPPOSITE PAGE:** *The whatnot, a smaller version of the étagère, was a miniature trinket museum.* **ABOVE:** *Wicker furniture is one of the most enduring items from the Victorian era. Several of the original styles are still being produced.*

# WINDOW DESIGN (EXTERIOR)

Victorian windows were affected by the ornamentation process. Sills were converted into entablatures with cornice moldings, frieze aprons, brackets, and architrave moldings. Side faces were given chamfered edges, profiled caps and bases, recessed and raised panels, incised ornament, and applied ornament. Lintels were converted into entablatures or into caps with fillets, molds, panels, and keystones. Canopies or hoods ornamented the caps of windows in Gothic Revival, Italianate, and Mansardic villas. Sash design, expressed in terms of the number of glass panes or "lights" in one sash "over" another (as in "eight-over-eight") depended on developments in the production of affordable large sheets of glass. During the late Victorian decades, it was possible for most homes to use large sheets of glass to provide a view unimpeded by muntins, also called sash bars or glazing bars. At the same time, a romantic longing for the little panes of late medieval and Colonial American sash resulted in muntin patterns called Queen Anne sash, often glazed with colored glass. Shutters and blinds, more often closed than open, were window components on homes lacking canopies or hoods, awnings, or interior shutters or blinds. Flyscreens, in use after the Civil War, were sometimes decorated in the gray of grisaille patterns or landscapes. Plain windows, especially those of the late Victorian period, had accented details, were given special sash colors, and sometimes had highlighted putty lines.

# WINDOW GARDENS

More gardens were made by Victorians inside windows than outside. "Window gardening," wrote Henry T. Williams in *Window Gardening for Parlor Decoration* (1871), "is one of the most elegant, satisfactory, yet least expensive of all departments of Rural Taste." Even the humblest Victorian cottage had a shelf upon which were arranged pots of geraniums, primroses, and azaleas. Windows on which more time and money were spent were filled with cases, stands, baskets, and plants until they resembled miniature conservatories.

# WOMEN'S COLLEGES

The greatest achievements in the field of Victorian education were public schools and women's colleges. The most famous early Victorian women's college, Mount Holyoke, was started in South Hadley, Massachusetts, by Mary Lyon in 1837, the year of Queen Victoria's coronation. College coeducation also began in 1837 at Oberlin in Ohio; Antioch, in Yellow Springs, Ohio, followed in 1852 and had as its first president "The Father of American Public Education," Horace Mann. The most famous high Victorian college for women was Vassar, in Poughkeepsie, New York, founded in 1865 by a brewer named Matthew Vassar, who had been influenced by the writings of Sarah Josepha Hale in her *Godey's Lady's Book*.

# WOOTON DESK

After all these years, the Wooton is still the undisputed king of desks. These desks, which were advertised as miniature portable countinghouses, were filing cabinet, mailbox, bookcase, and safe all in one. Wootons do everything but seal the deal and sign the checks; they roll, they fold up, they lock, and they could accommodate books, pencils, letters, correspondence, inkwells, ledgers, paper clips, and anything and everything else essential to enterprising businessmen like Jay Gould and J.D. Rockefeller, who each owned one. Patented in 1874, Wooton desks sold for enormous sums in those days. They are still the most expensive desks around.

▨ *Windows on Victorian houses were imbued with a lot of personality. They came in a variety of shapes and sizes and were often highly decorated both inside and outside.*

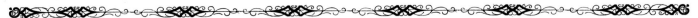

# Bibliography

## INTERIOR DECORATION

Alford, Lady A. *Needlework as Art*. Boston: Charles River Books, 1977.

Andere, Mary. *Old Needlework Boxes and Tools: Their Story and How to Collect Them*. New York: Drake, 1971.

Aslin, Elizabeth. *The Aesthetic Movement: Prelude to Art Nouveau*. New York: Praeger, 1969.

Audsley, George Ashdown. *Polychromatic Decoration*. London: H. Sotheran, 1882.

Baker, Cozy. *Kaleidoscope Renaissance*. Annapolis: Beechcliff Books, 1993.

Banham, Joanna, Sally MacDonald, and Julia Porter. *Victorian Interior Design*. London: Cassell Books, 1991.

Beecher, Catherine E., and Harriet Beecher Stowe. *American Woman's Home*. New York: J.B. Ford and Co., 1869.

Bishop, Robert, and Patricia Coblentz. *The World of Antiques, Art, and Architecture in Victorian America*. New York: Dutton, 1979.

Blumin, Leonard. *Victorian Decorative Art: A Photographic Study of Ornamental Design in Antique Doorknobs*. Mill Valley, Calif.: Victorian Design Press, 1983.

*Bulletin Philadelphia Art Museum*, 1989.

Cook, Clarence. *The House Beautiful*. New York: Scribner, 1881.

———. *What Shall We Do With Our Walls?* New York: Warren, Fuller & Lange, 1884.

Cooper, Diana, and Norman Battershill. *Victorian Sentimental Jewellery*. New York: David & Charles Newton Abbot, 1972.

Davenport, Millia. *The Book of Costume*, Volume II. New York: Crown, 1948.

Day, Louis F. *Art in Needlework*. Detroit: Singing Tree Press, 1971.

Dubrow, Eileen and Richard. *American Furniture of the 19th Century, 1840–1880*. Exton, Pa.: Schiffer Publishing Ltd., 1983.

Eastlake, Charles Locke. *Hints on Household Taste in Furniture, Upholstery and Other Details*. London: Longmans, Green, 1872.

Edis, Robert. *Decoration and Furniture of Town Houses*. London: C.K. Paul & Co., 1881.

Ewing, Elizabeth. *History of Children's Costume*. London: B.T. Batsford, 1977.

Felkin, William. *History of the Machine-Wrought Hosiery and Lace Manufacturers*. London: Longmans, Green, 1867.

Flower, Margaret. *Victorian Jewellery*. New York: Duell, Sloan and Pearce, 1951.

Godey, Louis Antoine, and Sarah Josepha Hale. *Godey's Lady Book*. New York: The Godey Company, 1830–1898.

Golovin, Anne Castrodale. "Bridgeport's Gothic Ornament: The Harral-Wheeler House." *Smithsonian Studies in History and Technology*, No. 18, 1972.

Groves, Sylvia. *The History of Needlework Tools and Accessories*. New York: Acro Publishing Company, 1973.

Haertig, Evelyn. *Antique Combs & Purses*. Carmel, Calif.: Gallery Graphics Press, 1983.

Halen, Widar. *Christopher Dresser*. Oxford: Phaidon, 1990.

Hall, Zillah. *Machine-Made Lace in Nottingham*. Nottingham City Museum and Art Gallery, 1964.

Hibberd, Shirley. *Rustic Adornments*. London: Groombridge & Sons, 1857.

Howe, Katherine S., David B. Warren, and Jane Badger Davies. *The Gothic Revival Style in America, 1830–1870*. Houston Museum of Fine Arts, 1976.

Jones, Owen. *The Grammar of Ornament*. London: Studio Editions, 1886.

Katzenberg, Dena D. *Baltimore Album Quilts*. Baltimore Museum of Art, 1981.

Lambton, Lucinda. *Temples of Convenience*. New York: St. Martin's Press, 1978.

Lichten, Frances. *Decorative Arts of Victoria's Era*. New York: Charles Scribner's Sons, 1950.

McLaughlin, M. Louise. *China Painting*. Cincinnati: R. Clarke & Co., 1877.

Miller, Andrew and Dalia. *Survey of American Clocks: Calendar Clocks*. Elgin, Ill.: Antiquatat, 1972.

Moss, Roger W. *Lighting for Historic Buildings*. Washington, D.C.: The Preservation Press, 1988.

Mowat, Alexander and William. *A Treatise on Stairbuilding and Handrailing*. London: G. Bell & Sons, 1900.

Nylander, Richard C. *Lighting Reproduction Wallpapers*. Washington, D.C.: The Preservation Press, 1983.

Oliver, Anthony. *The Victorian Staffordshire Figure: A Guide For Collectors*. London: Heinemann, 1971.

Oman, Charles C., and Jean Hamilton. *Wallpapers: A History and Illustrated Catalogue of The Victoria and Albert Museum*. London: Sotheby Publications, 1982.

Ormsbee, Thomas H. *Field Guide to American Victorian Furniture*. Boston: Little, Brown, 1952.

Perry, Ann. *Renaissance Revival Victorian Furniture*. Grand Rapids Art Museum, 1976.

Phillips, Louisa. "A Land of Bric-a-Brac." *Good Housekeeping*, 1888.

*Picture Book of Authentic Mid-Victorian Gas Lighting Fixtures: A Reprint of the Historic Mitchell, Vance & Co. Catalog, ca. 1876*. New York: Dover Publications Inc., 1984.

Proctor, Molly G. *Victorian Canvas Work: Berlin Wool Work*. London: Drake Publishing, 1972.

Pugh, P.D.G. *Staffordshire Portrait Figures and Allied Subjects of the Victorian Period*. London: Barrie and Jenkins, 1970.

Racinet, Albert Charles August. *Polychromatic Ornament*. London: H. Sotheran & Co., 1873.

Rainwater, Dorothy T. and H. Ivan. *American Silverplate*. Nashville, Tenn.: T. Nelson, 1972.

Revi, Albert Christian. *American Cut and Engraved Glass*. New York: T. Nelson, 1964.

Sloan, Samuel. *Homestead Architecture*. Philadelphia: Lippincott, 1861.

*Stairway Design* Catalog. A. Dickey & Co. of Boston, 1896.

Spofford, Harriet Elizabeth Prescott. *Art Decoration Applied to Furniture*. New York: Harper, 1878.

Talbert, Bruce J. *Examples of Ancient & Modern Furniture: Metalwork, Tapestries, Decorations, Etc.* Boston: J.R. Osgood, 1877.

———. *Gothic Forms Applied to Furniture, Metalwork and Decoration for Domestic Homes*. Boston: J.R. Osgood, 1873.

Tortora, Phyllis, and Keith Eubank. *A Survey of Historic Costume*. New York: Fairchild Publications, 1989.

*Victorian Lighting: The R.E. Dietz Catalogue*. Watkins Glen, N.Y.: American Life Foundation, 1982.

Walker, John and Elizabeth. *Pressed Glass in America: Encyclopedia of the First Hundred Years, 1825–1925.* Ivyland, Pa.: Antique Acres, 1985.

Walker, Mrs. L. *Instructive and Ornamental Paper Work.* New York: Charles Scribner's Sons, 1901.

Wallace, David H. *John Rogers: The People's Sculptor.* Middleton, Conn.: Wesleyan University Press, 1967.

Williams, Henry T. *Ornamental Designs for Fret-Work, Fancy Carving and Home Decorations.* New York: H.T. Williams, 1875–77.

Williams, Susan. *Savory Suppers and Fashionable Feasts: Dining in Victorian America.* New York: Pantheon Books, 1985.

Wilson, H. Weber. *Great Glass in American Architecture: Decorative Windows and Doors Before 1920.* New York: Dutton, 1986.

Winkler, Gail Caskey, and Roger W. Moss. *Victorian Interior Decoration, American Interiors 1830–1900.* New York: Henry Holt and Co., 1986.


## EXTERIOR DECORATION: ARCHITECTURE

Alexander, Edwin P. *Down at the Depot: American Railroad Stations from 1831 to 1920.* New York: Crown, 1970.

Archer, John. "Country and City in the American Romantic Suburb." *Journal of the Society of Architectural Historians,* May 1983.

Aslet, Clive. *The American Country House.* New Haven, Conn.: Yale University Press, 1990.

Badger, Daniel. *Illustrations of Iron Architecture Made by the Architectural Iron Works of the City of New York.* New York: Baker & Godwin, 1865.

Benjamin, Asher. *The Architect, or Practical House Carpenter.* Boston: L. Coffin, 1844.

Bunting, Bainbridge. *Houses of Boston's Back Bay, 1840–1917.* Cambridge, Mass.: Harvard University Press, 1967.

Burrows, T.H. *Pennsylvania School Architecture.* Harrisburg, Pa.: A.B. Hamilton, 1855.

Cleaveland, Henry, and Samuel Baccus. *Village and Farm Cottages.* New York: D. Appleton & Co., 1856.

Condit, Carl W. *The Chicago School of Architecture.* Chicago: University of Chicago Press, 1964.

Creese, Walter F. "Fowler and the Domestic Octagon." *Art Bulletin,* 1946.

Davies, Philip. *Splendors of the Raj: British Architecture in India, 1660–1947.* London: J. Murray, 1985.

Davis, Julia Finette. "International Expositions, 1851–1900." *American Association of Architectural Bibliographers Papers,* IV, 1967.

Downing, Andrew Jackson. *Cottage Residences.* New York: Wiley & Putnam, 1842.

Eastlake, Charles Locke. *History of the Gothic Revival.* London: Longmans, 1872.

Eliot, W.H. *A Description of the Tremont House.* Boston: Gray and Bowen, 1830.

Eveleth, Samuel F. *School-house Architecture.* New York: G.E. Woodward, 1870.

Fowler, Orson Squire. *A Home For All.* New York: S.R. Wells, 1853.

Freeman, John Crosby. "Historic Paint Colors." *Traditional Building,* May-June 1990.

———."Victorian Porch and Verandah Glossary." *Victorian Homes,* Summer 1991.

Gayle, Margot. *Cast-Iron Architecture in New York.* New York: Dover Publications, 1974.

———, David Look, and John Waite. *Metals in America's Historic Buildings.* Washington, D.C.: U.S. Department of the Interior, 1980.

Giedion, Sigried. *Space, Time and Architecture.* Cambridge, Mass.: Harvard University Press, 1941.

Girouard, Mark. *Sweetness and Light: The Queen Anne Movement 1860–1900.* Oxford: Clarendon Press, 1977.

Godey, Louis Antoine, and Sarah Josepha Hale. *Godey's Lady's Book.* New York: The Godey Company, 1830–1898.

Guilford, Andrew. *America's Country Schools.* Washington, D.C.: Preservation Press, 1984.

Gwilt, Joseph. *Encyclopedia of Architecture.* London: Longman, 1842.

Hitchcock, Henry-Russell. *The Architecture of H.H. Richardson and His Times.* New York: Museum of Modern Art, 1936.

———, and William Seale. *Temples of Democracy: The State Capitols of the U.S.A.* New York: HBJ, 1976.

Holland, Francis Ross, Jr. *America's Lighthouses: Their Illustrated History Since 1716.* Brattleboro, Vt.: S. Greene Press, 1972.

Horowitz, Hellen Lefkowitz. *Alma Mater: Design and Experience in Women's Colleges from Their 19th Century Beginnings to the 1930s.* New York: A.A. Knopf, 1984.

Ignatieff, Michael. *A Just Measure of Pain: The Penitentiary in the Industrial Revolution, 1750–1850.* New York: Pantheon, 1978.

Jandl, H. Ward, ed. *The Technology of Historic American Buildings: Studies of the Materials, Craft Processes, and the Mechanization of Building Construction.* Foundation for Preservation Technology, 1983.

Kahn, Renee, and Ellen Meagher. *Preserving Porches.* New York: Holt, 1990.

Kirkbride, Dr. Thomas S. *Remarks on the Construction and General Arrangements of Hospitals for the Insane* (pamphlet). Philadelphia: Lippincott, 1847.

Landau, Sarah Bradford. "Richard Morris Hunt, The Continental Picturesque, and the 'Stick Style.'" *Journal of the Society of Architectural Historians,* October 1983.

Lockwood, Charles. *Bricks and Brownstone: The New York Row House 1783–1929.* New York: McGraw-Hill, 1972.

Maass, John. *The Glorious Enterprise: The Centennial Exhibition of 1876.* Watkins Glen, N.Y.: American Life Books, 1973.

McArdle, Alma and Deirdre. *Carpenter Gothic: Nineteenth-Century Ornamented Houses of New England.* New York: Whitney Library of Design, 1978.

Meeks, Carroll L.V. *The Railroad Station: An Architectural History.* New Haven, Conn.: Yale University Press, 1956.

Moss, Roger W. *The American Country House.* New York: H. Holt, 1991.

Ochsner, Jeffrey Karl. "Architecture for the Boston and Albany Railroad: 1881–1894." *Journal of the Society of Architectural Historians,* June 1988.

———. *H.H. Richardson: Complete Architectural Works.* Cambridge, Mass.: M.I.T. Press, 1982.

O'Gorman, James F., ed. *H.H. Richardson and His Office: Selected Drawings.* Cambridge, Mass.: Harvard College Library, 1974.

Pare, Richard, ed. *Court House: A Photographic Document.* New York: Horizon Press, 1978.

Ranlett, William H. *The Architect*. New York: W.H. Graham, 1847.

Robinson, William. *Parks, Promenades, and Gardens of Paris Described and Considered in Relation to the Wants of Our Own Cities*. London: J. Murray, 1869.

Schmidt, Carl F. *The Octagon Fad*. Scottsville, N.Y.: 1958.

Scully, Vincent, Jr. *The Shingle Style and Stick Style: Architectural Theory and Design from Richardson to the Origins of Wright*. New Haven, Conn.: Yale University Press, 1971.

Shelgren, Olaf William. *Cobblestone Landmarks of New York State*. Syracuse, N.Y.: Syracuse University Press, 1978.

Shepard, Thomas A., and James Elmes. *Metropolitan Improvements*. London: Jones & Co., 1827.

Sprague, Paul E. "The Origin of Balloon Framing." *Journal of the Society of Architectural Historians*, 1981.

Stern, Robert A.M., ed. *The Anglo-American Suburb of The United States*. New York: St. Martin's Press, 1981.

Tinniswood, Adrian. *Historic Houses of The National Trust*. London: National Trust, 1991.

Turner, Paul Venable. *Campus: An American Planning Tradition*. Cambridge, Mass.: M.I.T. Press, 1984.

Vaux, Calvert. *Villas and Cottages*. New York: Harper, 1857.

Waite, Diana S. *Ornamental Ironwork: Two Centuries of Craftsmanship in Albany and Troy*. Albany, N.Y.: Mount Ida Press, 1990.

Warner, Sam Bass. *Streetcar Suburbs: The Process of Growth in Boston 1870–1900*. Cambridge, Mass.: Harvard University Press, 1978.

Zurier, Rebecca. *The American Firehouse: An Architectural and Social History*. New York: Abbeville Press, 1982.

## HORTICULTURAL DECORATION

Alphand, Adolphe. *Promenades of Paris*. Paris: J. Rothschild, 1868.

Andres, Edouard. *L'Art des Jardins, Traite Général de la Composition des Parcs et Jardins*. Paris: G. Masson, 1879.

Cook, Jack. "Your Back-Yard Fruit and Nut Orchard." *Country Journal*, May 1984.

Downing, Andrew Jackson. "A Chat in the Kitchen Garden." *Horticulturalist*, October 1849.

———. *Fruits and Fruit Trees of America*. New York: Wiley & Putnam, 1845.

Gaither, Robin. "Flowers Speak for the Heart." *Green Scene*, January 1988.

Henderson, Peter. *Practical Floriculture*. New York: O. Judd & Co., 1887.

Kunst, Scott G., and Arthur O. Tucker. "A Preliminary List of Origination Lists for Ornamental Plants." *APT (Association for Preservation Technology) Bulletin*, XXI, No. 2, 1989.

Rand, Edward Sprague. *Flowers for the Parlor and Garden*. Boston: J.E. Tilton & Co., 1864.

Robinson, William. *Parks, Promenades and Gardens of Paris Described and Considered in Relation to the Wants of Our Own Cities*. London: J. Murray, 1869.

Scott, Frank J. *Art of Beautifying Suburban Home Grounds*. New York: D. Appleton, 1870.

Vick, James. *Vick's Flower and Vegetable Garden*. Rochester, N.Y.: J. Vick, 1878.

Waterman, Catherine. *Flora's Lexicon*. Boston: Phillips Sampson, 1852.

Weidenmann, Jacob. *Beautifying Country*. New York: O. Judd & Co., 1870.

Williams, Henry T. *Window Gardening*. New York: H.T. Williams, 1871.

## MISCELLANEOUS

Alcott, Louisa May. *An Old-Fashioned Girl*. New York: Dell, 1987.

Anscombe, Isabelle. *Arts & Crafts Style*. New York: Rizzoli, 1991.

Aslin, Elizabeth. *The Aesthetic Movement: Prelude to Art Nouveau*. New York: F.A. Praeger, 1969.

*Bloomingdale's Illustrated 1886 Catalog*. New York: Dover Publications Inc., 1988.

De Vries, Leonard. *Victorian Inventions*. London: J. Murray, 1971.

Duncan, Alastair. *Masterworks of Louis Comfort Tiffany*. New York: Harry N. Abrams, 1989.

Fendelman, Helaine, and Jeri Schwartz. *The Official Price Guide Holiday Collectibles*. New York: Balantine Books, 1991.

Hardy, William. *A Guide to Art Nouveau Style*. Secaucus, N.J.: Chartwell Books, 1986.

Hosley, William. *The Japan Idea: Art and Life in Victorian America*. Hartford: Wadsworth Atheneum, 1990.

Howell, Peter. *The Victorian House Catalogue*. New York: Sterling Publishing, 1992.

Mace, O. Henry. *Collector's Guide to Victoriana*. Radnor, Pa.: Chilton Book Co., 1991.

Maisak, N.C. *Smart Buyer's Guide to Antiques*. Haupauge, N.Y.: Seventh String Press, 1991.

McCabe, James D. *Illustrated History of the Centennial Exhibition: A Collector's Reprint*. Philadelphia: National Publishing Co., 1975.

Metropolitan Museum of Art. *In Pursuit of Beauty, Americans and the Aesthetic Movement*. New York: Rizzoli, 1986.

Meyer, Priscilla S. *Victorian Detail: A Working Dictionary*. Armonk, N.Y.: P.S. Meyer, 1980.

*Montgomery Ward & Co. 1895 Catalog*. New York: Dover Publications Inc., 1969.

Mountbatten-Windsor, Sarah (the Duchess of York), and Benita Stoney. *Victoria and Albert: A Family Life at Osborne House*. London: Weidenfeld & Nicolson, 1991.

Phillips, Susan S., ed. *Charmed Places, Hudson Rover Artists and Their Houses, Studios and Vistas*. New York: Harry N. Abrams, 1988.

St. Marie, Satenig, and Carolyn Flaherty. *Romantic Victorian Weddings, Then and Now*. New York: New American Library & Dutton Studio Books, 1992.

Siegler, Burnedett M. *The Sphinx and the Lotus: The Egyptian Movement in American Decorative Arts 1865–1935*. Yonkers, N.Y.: The Hudson River Museum, 1990.

Volpe, Tod M., and Beth Cathers. *Treasures of the American Arts and Crafts Movement, 1890–1920*. London: Thames and Hudson, 1988.

Wilhide, Elizabeth. *William Morris, Decor and Design*. New York: Harry N. Abrams, 1991.

# *Index*

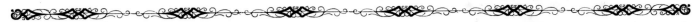

**FRONT MATTER PHOTOGRAPHY**

© Edward Addeo: p. 10
© Gross and Daley: p. 6
© Nancy Hill p.2
© Keith Scott Morton: p.9

**PHOTOGRAPHY CREDITS FOR SILHOUETTES:**

Courtesy of the Bombay
    Company: **pp.12, 94** right;
Courtesy of American Life
    Foundation: **p.45** right;
Courtesy of Joan Bogart
    Antiques: **pp.15** right, **135**,
Photography by Sheree Brown:
    **p.158**;
Courtesy of Christie's: **p.185**;
© Gross and Daley: **p.20**;
Courtesy of Neal Auction
    Company, New Orleans: **p.26**;
© Randy O'Rourke: **p.127**;
Palubniak Picture Archive:
    **pp.109, 171**;
© David Phelps: **p.172**;
Courtesy of Renovator's Design:
    **p.99** left;
Courtesy of the Shelburne
    Museum: **p.14**;
Courtesy of Stingray Hornsby
    Antiques: **pp.49** left, **79, 80,
    97** both, **106** bottom, **113**
    right, **117** right, **157** top;
Courtesy of Thonet: **p.35** both;
Courtesy of Victorian Papers;
Photography by Deborah
    Springer: **p.123**